FOUND

True Stories *from*
TRAVELERS REST, SOUTH CAROLINA

Published in Beaverton, Oregon, by Good Catch Publishing.
www.goodcatchpublishing.com
V1.1

Printed in the United States of America

Table of Contents

DEDICATION

We dedicate this book to all who seek something
more from life, something with meaning, something
beyond the daily routine, something that doesn't leave
you wanting or unfulfilled. May our stories inspire you to
find what you've been looking for all along.

ACKNOWLEDGEMENTS

I would like to thank Rob Rucci for his vision for this book and for his hard work in making it a reality. To the people of Upcountry, thank you for your boldness and vulnerability in sharing your personal stories.

This book would not have been published without the amazing efforts of our project manager and editor, Hayley Pandolph. Her untiring resolve pushed this project forward and turned it into a stunning victory. Thank you for your great fortitude and diligence. Deep thanks to our incredible editor in chief, Michelle Cuthrell, and executive editor, Jen Genovesi, for all the amazing work they do. I would also like to thank our invaluable proofreader, Melody Davis, for the focus and energy she has put into perfecting our words.

Lastly, I want to extend our gratitude to the creative and very talented Jenny Randle, who designed the beautiful cover for *Found: True Stories from Travelers Rest, South Carolina.*

Daren Lindley
President and CEO
Good Catch Publishing

The book you are about to read
is a compilation of authentic life stories.
The facts are true, and the events are real.
These storytellers have dealt with crisis, tragedy, abuse
and neglect and have shared their most private moments,
mess-ups and hang-ups in order for others to learn and
grow from them. In order to protect the identities of those
involved in their pasts, the names and details of some
storytellers have been withheld or changed.

INTRODUCTION

Everyone is searching for something — be it happiness, peace, security, enduring love or some other noble objective. It is the search that drives us, propelling us forward through life, shaping our choices, determining our direction.

Some form new relationships in the hope of finding contentment through human connection. Others in vocational pursuits search for that which will ultimately satisfy. Still others seek solace in their affinity for what they have attained, however temporary that satisfaction may be. Regardless of the pursuit, we are all searching.

The pages that follow contain seven true stories of searching people. These are individuals from different walks of life, following different paths, seeking answers to different questions. Every journey is unique, yet what lies in the soul of each one is the common desire for that which truly fulfills, a common desire that inspires us to act, to push on in search of the final answer to our greatest longing.

These are remarkable accounts of real people, yet they are the stories of all of us, a collection of seven true tales that describe the yearning of every human heart. Seven stories full of heartache and happiness, seven adventures fraught with failure and success, real people who finally found what they were looking for all along.

PLAY ON
The Story of Ian
Written by Marty Minchin

The blinding stage lights blurred most of the massive crowd spread out in front of me, but the faces I could make out stared raptly at the stage. I nodded to Derek, my bassist, and hit the first chord on my guitar. The sound rang through the open air, and the crowd screamed its approval as we launched into our opening song.

I flipped my long hair over my shoulder, already damp with sweat from the heavy night air. A wall of sound — drums, bass, vocals — surrounded us as I banged my head to the beat and strutted around the stage.

I AM A ROCK STAR.

I lost myself in the bliss of a dream materializing around me. The crazy fans, the adoration, the songs I'd written coming to life on this stage.

With one last flourish on the guitar, The VP's set was over. I leapt off the stage like I was jumping into a pot of gold, basking in dreams of a music future that would surely be as bright as those lights behind me.

Backstage, Kansas waited to come on. We had just opened for one of the biggest bands in the American rock world.

There was nowhere else to go but up.

FOUND

འའའ

My parents settled outside Joplin, Missouri, after I was born, and I spent my childhood riding dirt bikes and taking care of our horses. My dad worked as a diesel mechanic, and my mom — who was a better carpenter than most men — usually held down a factory job. My half-siblings, both from my parents' previous marriages, were enough older than me that I was pretty much an only child, and in our rural homestead, I had to be my own best friend. After school, I watched cartoons or *Gilligan's Island* and fixed myself a tomato and mayonnaise sandwich.

We moved 25 miles into Joplin when I was 12, and for the first time I could walk around a neighborhood and see other kids. We boys played football in the park and chased girls, though we wouldn't have known what to do if we actually caught one. The days seemed to float by lazily, a stream of school and friends, but the thoughts in my head always seemed to be racing like cars on a speed track. My brain didn't turn off at bedtime, and I'd often lie in my bed at night and follow my wandering thoughts. Sometimes I'd solve world hunger. Other times I'd build a rocket ship. I grasped the information I learned at school, but homework and taking notes bored me. I drew instead, sketching the tanks and machines guns and crashing airplanes that materialized in my head. Sometimes I scribbled the names of bands I'd like to be in.

I assumed the role of guitar-playing dude early on in life. Music, I like to say, chose me.

PLAY ON

Mom loved to sing and play her guitar. She'd pick what we called "hootenanny songs" out of those old Gospel songbooks, and we'd sit around the kitchen table with our friends and sing our hearts out. We sang "I Saw the Light," "Little Brown Church" and countless other songs about God and life in America. If I had a favorite song of the moment, my mom would play it for me, over and over.

I was giving concerts before I went to kindergarten, strumming a canoe paddle and dancing across the living room rug like I was Elvis singing rock and roll to a throng of adoring fans. When Mom got tired of me asking to play her guitar, she bought me a beat-up old electric guitar with four strings. By age 4, I could regularly be found sitting in front of my record player, moving the needle back over and over until I knew the melody well enough to pick it out on my guitar. When she thought I was old enough, Mom taught me to play chords.

My organized music career started in middle school band with the sousaphone, a brass instrument that's as big and unwieldy as its cousin, the tuba. The band director, who apparently had extreme halitosis, corrected my mistakes by spinning my sousaphone's mouthpiece around to face her, playing the correct notes and returning the mouthpiece to its original position. I tried not to let the wave of disgust show on my face when I blew into the now-stinky mouthpiece.

The musicians in the corner of the room looked like they were having a lot more fun.

FOUND

"Hey," I asked the director after one week of sousaphone torture, "can I play drums?"

I learned percussion on a snare drum we found at a pawnshop, and the radio continued to be my de facto teacher as I picked out songs and dreamed that I was not only playing the music, but playing on stage *with* the musicians. By seventh grade, my best friend and I started our own band.

Our moms allowed us to alternate practices between our two houses, and by the end of the year, Mom got us our first gig: playing the holiday party at the facility for people with mental handicaps where she worked.

We each earned $5, and despite our less-than-awesome skill level, the enthusiastic crowd clad in Elvis T-shirts danced around happily to "Smoke on the Water," "Johnny B. Goode" and anything else we played with a beat.

Not long after, a girl at school broke my heart, giving me the occasion to write my first sappy love song. The tune didn't launch my music career, but I was getting better at playing the guitar. I would almost say I was obsessed with it.

I joined another band as a guitarist, covering songs by The Doobie Brothers and Toto. I tried sports and liked weight lifting, but music was my thing.

My dad was strict about how long I could talk on the phone in case someone else was trying to call in, so I didn't spend a lot of time chatting with friends and girlfriends. I preferred to pick up my guitar, put on an album and play along with it until I learned the songs by ear.

While I was working my way through high school, my dad was battling a diagnosis of prostate cancer that originally gave him six months to live.

After chemotherapy and other treatments, he went into remission, but when I was 17, he fell into a coma and never came out. He died on Mother's Day.

My mom was a strong woman. She'd gotten my dad's attention by what would be considered stalking today, visiting him at the auto repair shop where he worked and hanging around until he agreed to get coffee with her. She always worked, and after Dad died she got a job at a home for girls with mental handicaps. She pretty much lived there, which left me on my own at home. Playing my guitar had always been way more fun than school, so the showroom of the local guitar shop became my classroom. My best friend and I wiled away the hours playing the guitar, and when I saved up enough money from the part-time jobs I'd held since I was 13, I traded in my beaters and secondhand guitars and bought my first serious, professional-grade guitar.

With an income also came the means to buy alcohol, and on the weekends my buddies and I would hand over some cash to an older kid who would buy us beer and wine. Our weekend entertainment revolved around getting drunk, which seemed like the normal teenage thing to do.

FOUND

‟‟‟

I knew, however, that my future wasn't necessarily in Joplin. A few big fish in the music industry were circling. A record label was interested in one of the bands I was playing for, and I'd won several guitar-playing contests. At age 20, I decided to take my guitar and move on — and out — of Missouri. I'd signed with a referral agency and interviewed with a couple of gigs before choosing a Christian band based in South Carolina.

Christianity wasn't foreign to me. I'd always believed in God, and my family occasionally visited a nearby Baptist church on a Sunday morning. I was too restless to sit still and focus on the sermons, but I couldn't get enough of the Bible stories my grandmother would read me from her King James Bible. I loved to listen to her voice telling the tales of Moses, Abraham and Noah in the formal English of the 17th century.

I met God myself one night. That's the best way I can describe it. As usual, the night was passing much more slowly than my brain was moving, flitting from one idea to the next. The quiet offered too much space for my thoughts to roam, so I flipped on the TV in my room to add some noise as I rolled my Hot Wheels toy cars back and forth on the rug. The only thing on at 2 a.m. was a television evangelist boisterously talking about God.

The TV preacher's words didn't really register with me, but something more palpable did. An invisible presence seemed to lay its hands on my shoulders, the light but firm touch of the God who occupied the King James Bible, my mother's unwavering faith and even the guy on the TV.

I dropped the Hot Wheel and looked up.

God, I want to get to know you. My young mind focused for a moment on the only thing that mattered. *I want to be saved like that preacher is talking about.*

All by myself that night, I asked God to forgive me for the things I had done wrong. I asked him to be my friend. It would be years before God and I would meet this way again, but I always knew that he was there.

My mom loved to talk about God. She read the Bible all of the time and taught me what she learned. She was unshakable and strong, and the day I drove away from Joplin, she stood in the driveway with her arms crossed across her chest as I loaded up my music equipment. I threw my clothes into the backseat, almost as an afterthought.

It was time to go.

"Let me pray for you first." Mom walked over and rested her hand on my shoulder.

"God, be with Ian as he drives south and into a new life. Walk beside him, and keep him safe. Help him to use his musical gifts the best that he can. Stay close to him on the road so that he arrives safely in South Carolina."

She gently squeezed my arm, and we opened our eyes and looked at each other.

"I love you, Ian. You're going to be great." Mom smiled.

She tipped up on her toes and kissed me on the forehead.

"Call me when you get there."

I slid into the driver's seat, rolled down the window and began the long drive southeast.

I spent one night outside Greenville, South Carolina, in Travelers Rest. The tiny town was once a Native American settlement and got its English name due to its popularity as a rest stop for weary travelers and teamsters driving animals before they made the difficult trek into the Blue Ridge Mountains. The town served the same purpose for me — after one night of sleep and a day of rehearsals with my new band, we boarded the tour bus and hit the road for a string of concerts and, for me, a fresh start.

The guys in the band didn't drink, and instead of partying, they held Bible studies. It felt good to live the clean life, away from the drinking and partying I'd fallen into in Joplin.

However, the rock star life called to me like the siren of Greek mythology who lured the sailors to their death with her music. I enjoyed my 18 months with the Christian band, but in the end, I jumped off the ship and swam toward that intoxicating rock song.

అంఅంఅం

"It doesn't get any better than this, does it?" I grinned at Derek, my bassist, as our crew finished sound checks. My longtime best friend, with whom I'd been writing songs for years, had started The VP with me and knew exactly what I meant.

The look that passed between us carried the knowledge that we were once two guys teaching music to kids at the same music store in Joplin. Now I was a rock star, hair down to my butt and a closet filled with spandex. We had tour buses, guitars, alcohol and all the women we wanted.

We were standing together on the top of the figurative mountain we'd climbed together in the rock world, poised for the next peak. The VP was regularly featured in trade magazines and newspapers. We played for a crowd of 12,500, opening for Lynyrd Skynyrd. When I went home to Joplin, people would come to the music store to watch me try out guitars. A few days after opening for Kansas, we were scheduled to go into a studio and start recording a new album with a big-name record label.

That night with Kansas, we played like we'd never played before. The sound was impeccable. The crowd stayed with us until the last note. When the set was over, we joined the front row to rock with the headliners.

"Wow." I looked at Derek, shaking my head almost in disbelief that this was our life.

"I know," he said, smiling back. The thousands of hours of practice, the countless days in the studio and traveling across the United States playing were crystallizing into one perfect night.

And the next day, I was sure, would only get better.

FOUND

꙰ ꙰ ꙰

The phone rang in my apartment the next morning, the sound of a dream about to shatter.

"Hello?" I was groggy from the night before.

"Ian? It's Derek."

His voice was flat and lifeless.

"What's up? Everything okay?" I tried to buoy him up with my own lingering giddiness from the night before. We had just played the show of our life, for Pete's sake! We'd partied with Kansas!

"I don't want to do this anymore," he blurted out.

I digested that remark in silence for a moment.

"You're kidding with me, right?"

"No, man. I just can't. I wanna do something else."

Derek rambled on with some inexplicable reasoning that made no sense to me. The telephone receiver turned into a giant straw, and Derek's words were sucking the very essence of *me* out of my body. I was not just Ian Butler. I was the guitar player for The VP. Everything I lived, breathed or felt was about the band. If Derek quit, our contracts with the record label were null and void. The VP would be defunct.

I hung up the phone and slumped onto my couch as the energy drained out of me like a slow leak. My dreams, my future, deflated like a bike tire with a big nail stuck in it.

꙰ ꙰ ꙰

PLAY ON

I decided to go back to Joplin and start a business building and repairing guitars, a skill I'd learned in Travelers Rest at a little guitar shop.

A clean break with the rock star life, however, was impossible, and the trappings of the prior few years bumped along behind my car like cans tied to the bumper of a newlywed's getaway vehicle.

As I'd morphed into The Guitarist for The VP, I'd forgotten how to be myself. In fact, I'd never been comfortable in my own skin, and I found I needed a few beers to help me relax. Alcohol calmed my brain down, and if I drank enough my mind would shut off at night and allow me to sleep.

There also was the problem of my girlfriend, who had a 2-year-old daughter and was living with me. Things had not been going well between us, so moving to Missouri would be a convenient out.

"The band's over," I told her. Acting like a cold, heartless jerk made it easier. "I'm moving back to Missouri. If you want to come, that's great. If you don't, that's fine, too."

Stacy had a good job in retail and a company car. There's no way, I thought, that she would give that up.

"Okay, that's fine."

I did a double take. So much for setting out on my own into a new happily ever after.

"All right. I'm leaving in a few days."

My mom wouldn't let me live in her house in Joplin with a girl I wasn't married to, so Stacy and I got married.

FOUND

I became a stepfather at age 24, and my guitar business soon had more work than I could manage.

I didn't know how to be a dad to Stacy's daughter. I loved the little girl, but I'd given up drinking and consumed myself with work in its place. I slowly disengaged myself from my new family, untangling any threads that bound us together as I spent more time in my guitar studio and less time with them. I longed to separate myself, to feel nothing. Sometimes, sitting in my van at a stoplight, I'd think about suicide.

Turning back to old habits, I renewed my relationship with beer. I'd grab a few out of the refrigerator after work on my way through the house to my home studio. The solitude was comforting, and I played and fixed guitars long into the night.

When Stacy became pregnant with our son Evan, she gave me the reverse of the ultimatum I'd given her not too long ago: She was going back to her mother in South Carolina. I could come, or I could stay in Missouri.

"That's my boy in your belly!" I shouted. "You can't leave!"

The look she gave me said otherwise.

We rented a house in South Carolina, and my plan was to commute six hours to Nashville and play guitar on tour with a songwriter friend of mine. I'd be on the bus for two weeks and then have a week off at home.

But as Stacy's pregnant belly grew bigger, something snapped in me. Overwhelmed with panic, I needed a new direction in my life. I had kids, a wife and bills to pay.

PLAY ON

I decided I was done with music. The rock star dream was dead, and I needed to bury it.

❧❧❧

I sold all of my guitars, keeping only the old 1940s-era guitar that my mom played when I was a kid. Playing guitar had once been like breathing to me, but I had to find a new source of oxygen. I needed a real job, and I needed to focus on my family.

I got hired as a marketing representative and worked my way into management. I wore a suit and took marketing courses. When I got home from work, I downed three quick shots of bourbon that made me pliable, able to float through the rest of the day like an agreeable piece of driftwood.

Stacy and I struggled. We had separated once, and our ongoing efforts to keep it together were like Band-Aids on a gash that needed stitches.

"What in the world is this?" I called out to Stacy one afternoon as I pulled a plastic baggie out of the pocket of an old coat I'd dug out of the back of the closet.

"Pot. What do you think?" Stacy knew that I recognized the crumbled, dried leaves in the bag.

"How long have you been smoking this? You know I don't like it!" No matter how much I drank, I'd always been dead set against smoking marijuana, probably due to the bygone days of growing up with my strict mom.

Stacy shrugged. "A while."

FOUND

My anger soon flowed away. Stacy wasn't going to quit, and I did like the idea of another substance that could bring on the numbness I craved. Soon we ended every evening smoking a joint in our bed, and Stacy's belly was growing again with a surprise pregnancy. She kept smoking through her pregnancy because the pot helped her eat despite severe nausea.

"Ian, get in here!"

I rushed to the bedroom. Stacy's hysterics were normal, but something different was in her voice.

"I'm bleeding. Oh, my God. The baby."

Jackson was due in six weeks. This was too early.

Stacy couldn't stop vomiting, and the bleeding continued. She lay listlessly on the bed, pale and limp, and I was afraid to move her.

"Stacy, I'm going to call an ambulance." She nodded weakly.

Jackson was born two weeks later, and he spent his first month of life in the hospital as Department of Social Services workers conducted an investigation into the pot the EMTs smelled in our bedroom that night. We took parenting classes, and Stacy was investigated for smoking pot while pregnant. I beat myself up. *What kind of father am I? I let this happen!*

The truth was, I loved my kids more than I loved Stacy. I loved to play with them, and I got up every morning and fixed their breakfast and got them off to school. I did their homework with them at night.

Trying to work things out with Stacy felt like pushing

over a brick wall. I invited her to an outdoor music festival on her birthday in a last-ditch attempt to reconcile. It was Memorial Day weekend, and the festival promised some great music. All I wanted was for things to be right between us.

Conversation remained stilted as we walked through the fair. Out of nowhere, she took a jab at me.

I wilted. The tone of her voice said what her words didn't. *I hate you. Leave me alone.*

Overwhelmed with hopelessness, I turned and faded into the crowd, leaving Stacy behind. I weaved through people holding hands, laughing, swaying to the live music, on my way out the festival's gate and onto a main street in Spartanburg. The street was lit with car headlights and streetlamps, but the businesses were dark at 11 p.m.

I stopped at a pay phone and called my friend.

"Hey, Ian! What's going on?"

"Not much. Just wanted to say hi. Stacy and I were at the festival."

"How was it?"

"Pretty good. I'm headed out now."

"Okay." I knew he was wondering why I had called. I wasn't going to tell him it was just to hear a familiar voice, to make one last human connection.

"Okay, man. Good talking to you. I'll see you." I hung up.

My plan was to swallow a bottle of Dramamine and drink a six-pack of beer. After downing the pills and two beers, though, I was hungry. Waffle House was in walking distance, so I deemed that my final meal would be a Waffle House chicken melt, my favorite. Then I'd just walk out of the restaurant, down the road into the night and hopefully fall over into a ditch and never wake up.

Festival night meant Waffle House was busy, and it seemed to take an eternity to get a table and get my food. It took so long that the fall I'd planned for the ditch happened into my chicken melt instead.

"Wake up!"

My body was moving. I could feel the speed as the vehicle turned and swerved. My eyes swam and then focused on the stranger hovering above me, pounding my chest, startling me over and over again as I drifted in and out of consciousness.

"Come on! Wake up!"

ৡৡৡ

"Look, I wasn't trying to kill myself, okay?"

The psychiatrist looked at me skeptically, unblinking, pen poised to take notes on a clipboard.

"Sir, you had a stomach full of Dramamine. Can you explain that?"

I constructed a new history for myself, lie by lie. I'd spent two weeks in the psyche ward at Patrick Harris State Hospital, where nurses wouldn't even let me keep the shoelaces in my shoes and where I tried to blend into the wall so the other residents wouldn't notice me.

"I was just tired, and my stomach was upset. You've

got to believe me. Maybe I lost count of how many pills I had taken."

She sat silently, so I continued.

"I have a lot to live for. I have a wife and three kids who need their dad. My new baby is only 8 months old! I have a great job, a great family and I would never leave them. There is no reason in the world for me to commit suicide. All I want to do is go home to my family. Please."

It worked. I went home, but my depression came with me. My marriage was broken beyond repair, and that nagging feeling that I couldn't put my finger on turned out to be my wife's secret boyfriend. I figured she'd just been biding her time until I'd inadvertently given her a good enough reason to leave.

ॐॐॐ

I picked up my old friend the guitar, quit my marketing job and settled into the life of a struggling musician. After a few months of sleeping on a friend's couch, I saved up some money from playing late-night acoustic gigs in bars and moved into an awful one-bedroom apartment. I slept on a blow-up mattress and drove a beat-up old car. I smoked pot and drank alcohol like it was water. I eventually bought a TV, and a friend gave me a kitchen table and an old couch.

The apartment started to feel like home, and my favorite guitar store offered me a job doing sales and repairs. I made some extra cash playing in bar bands almost every night, usually going home early in the morning with a woman I'd met at the show.

Life was rocking.

కింకింక

The first thing I noticed about Annie was her smile, quickly followed by her figure. She visited the guitar store enough that she was like everyone's little sister. She'd studied music with a master teacher, and I admired the way she played the guitar. I enjoyed her quick wit and great sense of humor, and we became fast friends. Sometimes she'd stop by the store to watch me fix guitars, and she and her friends often came to my shows. Wherever Annie showed up, she brought a ray of sunshine with her.

Even though she was wise beyond her years, however, Annie was still in college. She was a kid, and that's how I looked at her.

Six months into our friendship, though, I began to look at her differently. That, I knew, had to stop immediately. I was 37 years old, and Annie was 21.

"Annie, can we talk for a minute?" We had just come out of the movie theater, and it felt too risky for us to be together.

"Look, I think it would be a good idea for us to stop hanging out. I know we've been friends for a while, but I'm starting to feel more than friendly about you. Can you imagine if I met your dad? I mean, I could be your dad!

You're his only daughter, and he'd basically shoot me. This is never going to work. You've got to find someone your own age."

Annie looked like she wanted to punch me.

"Are you kidding me? All the guys my age are d***** bags."

We talked and talked, both of us wanting the same thing but knowing the 16-year age difference could cause problems. People would think I was dating a kid. They might think she had daddy issues.

Even though people constantly surrounded me, whether I was at work or at a bar, I felt weighed down by loneliness. Annie became a genuine friend during my stormy, self-medicated depression, and I cared deeply for her.

Because of a tumultuous home situation, she often studied for her college classes at the two-bedroom apartment I'd upgraded to. Sometimes when she took a break, we'd play the guitar together. The first time she came over after we'd decided to date, I gave her a gentle kiss goodnight before she left.

For the first time in a long time, I talked to God.

You know, I don't know if you are up there, but if you are, I pray that you would show me what to do. I like Annie. I think I love her. But I want to do what's right.

I handed this precious new relationship over to a God I hardly knew. That summer, after Annie hung out with my family at a Fourth of July party, we sat across the street from the airport and watched a glorious fireworks display.

FOUND

A path seemed to be opening up before us, and we knew from then on we'd be together.

ھەھەھ

When the waitress cleared our dinner plates, I placed a small black box on the table across from Annie.

"What's this?" she asked, giving me a sideways look. She knew what I was going to ask.

"Annie, will you marry me?"

Her eyes widened as I slid the box across the table. She slowly opened it, then snapped the lid shut and started laughing.

"You little jerk!" She tossed the box back to me. I'd bought her gold strap locks for her guitar, which matched the gold hardware on the instrument.

"Okay, okay." Annie was a girl who could take a joke.

I pulled the ring I'd saved up for out of my pants pocket and asked again.

"Yes," she said, smiling as I slid the ring on her finger.

Annie and I had moved into a house that I'd rented for her, me and Mom, who I'd talked into moving to South Carolina. Mom had developed chronic lung disease, and I wanted to make sure she got the best care possible.

Two weeks after I proposed to Annie, I went with Mom to the doctor for some follow-ups to lab work. The young doctor was kind, and he liked my mom a lot.

"The results turned up some additional problems," he began, his eyes full of compassion, then tears. "We found a mass in your lung ..."

The words blurred. "Lung cancer ... inoperable ... six months to live." Time stood still in the doctor's office. The doctor and I were crying.

Mom, ever the port in the storm, took the doctor's hand. "It's okay, honey," she assured him, giving me the same look. "You don't need to worry about me. I'll be with Jesus."

Mom hung on to her strength for about a month. I limited my odd jobs and gigs to stay at home and care for her.

She knocked on my door one morning before I left for work to ask a question. I stood in the door and watched as she shuffled away, hanging on to the full length of the back of the couch as she made her way across the living room. Mom was superwoman to me, a spiritual, emotional and physical stronghold who never seemed upset about the cancer that was killing her. She was deteriorating before my eyes, her clothes hanging off of her thin frame.

Mom handled her dying much better than I did. Three months after her diagnosis, I became her full-time caregiver. She needed a wheelchair to get around, and she liked me to push her around the yard while she told me all of the family stories that I hadn't been old enough to hear as a child. She liked to write letters, and she read her Bible every day. Despite her pallor and frailty, she never complained or even cried, except for one morning.

"Mom, what's wrong?" I'd cooked her breakfast eggs the way she liked them and brought them to her in bed. She was bawling like a baby.

"I just feel like I'm not doing enough," she said, sniffling.

"Are you crazy? Mom, you're bedridden!" Mom's cancer had progressed into an advanced stage, and her body swelled, and her functions slowed down. She had to sit up to sleep, propping herself up as she slowly drowned in the awfulness of cancer.

"Really, Mom. What do you mean you're not doing enough? How can that be possible?"

I could barely make out her words through her blubbering. "I don't think …" I waited for her to continue. "I just don't think I'm doing enough to tell people how wonderful Jesus is."

"Oh, Mom!" I hugged her carefully, laughing with relief that her grief was so wrapped up in something beautiful. "I think you're doing just fine!"

When Mom could talk on the phone, she called people to tell them about Jesus. If all she was up for was writing, she penned letters and emails. She couldn't wait to get to heaven, which she told me would be "awesome," and she needed to tell everyone she could while she was on earth about the Jesus she'd see there.

Annie and I moved our wedding date up to June 19, 2005, so that Mom could be there. The pastor at a church we sometimes attended performed the ceremony in our living room. In the pictures from that day, Mom looked so happy. My half-sister and her family came from Maryland, and our house filled with people and joy.

By September, Mom looked so puffy that all I could

think of was that she looked like a lion in the face. She and I had a good laugh about that.

About 2 a.m. on a Sunday morning in October, I went to her room to administer her breathing treatment. She was gone.

"Mommy!" I screamed, just like I had when I was a 3 year old and called for her out of fear and desperation. I thought I'd prepared myself for this moment, which I knew was coming. But nothing had prepared me for the finality of death, for my beloved, strong, joyful mom to be truly gone.

కాకాకా

Taking care of my mom full time had been costly. She needed breathing treatments and medication every four hours, and my sleep cycle was in disarray. I could barely function, even with an afternoon nap, and I drank to stay numb to the encroaching depression. I stumbled around for several months after Mom died, trying to reason out what had happened in my head.

By that time I was drinking a liter of vodka a day, trying not to feel anything. I couldn't think, didn't want to play the guitar and barely held it together. I submerged myself so deeply into a pool of self-pity that I failed to see that I had a beautiful wife, regular time with my kids and a decent job. I sputtered through life, refueling myself with alcohol every chance I got. I sat alone in my van under a shade tree at lunch, eating a cup of noodles and washing it down with vodka. I regularly woke up at night to have a drink so that my body could relax enough to keep sleeping.

☙☙☙

My boss laid me off after two years. He didn't say why, but I'm sure my drinking problem was obvious. I didn't even have a high school diploma, so my options were to go back on the road to play rock and roll or to start filling out job applications. I picked up my pen.

A friend from the Christian band I'd played for long before said he could help. A friend of his worked for a party rental business that set up big tents for weddings and other outside events.

"I can get you a job," he said. "It will be the worst job you've ever had, but you'll have steady work."

I was game.

There's nothing quite as pathetic as an out-of-shape alcoholic dragging heavy poles and tarps onto a lawn and struggling to assemble them into a tent. Even my boss took pity on me.

"You're just not as effective as the younger guys."

No kidding, I thought.

"I think we're going to move you to the kitchen."

The kitchen was as miserable as the outdoor setup, but at least washing the millions of cups and plates from each event was less physically demanding.

An unexpected phone call from an old friend in the music business saved me.

"We've got a position that we need someone with your talents to fill," he said. By talents, he meant my skills with selling and fixing guitars. He worked for Taylor, one of the biggest and most respected guitar companies in the world.

I was given the opportunity to audition for a job that encompasses all of the skills I'd mastered in my life — marketing, sales, music, instrument repair.

"We have six candidates, but you're the first person I thought of. This is a new position for Taylor, and you need to come up with a proposal for how you'd run this new division."

Taylor flew me to California, where I presented them with Excel spreadsheets, detailed plans and a proposal for their business venture. Two weeks later I turned in my notice to the worst job in the world because I'd gotten the best job I could have dreamed of.

My boss wasn't surprised.

"You know, Ian, I knew when you walked in the door for the first time that you didn't belong here. I didn't know where you were when you came here, but I think you know where you're going now."

I smiled. I certainly did.

अ>अ>अ>

My job with Taylor required me to travel at least four days a week to neighboring states, where I visited stores that sold Taylor guitars. I traveled with a tool kit and string kit to do warranty repairs. My traveling companion was my favorite guitar, which I always planned to play during downtime in the hotel. Instead, it sat in the corner in its case in hotel room after hotel room, rarely seeing the light of day. If I did take the instrument out, it had no appeal.

"Eh, not right now," I'd mutter to myself, as I'd place the guitar back in its case and pour myself one drink, and then another, until I passed out.

ॐॐॐ

As the beautiful green hills of Tennessee flashed by my van's window on Interstate 75, I grabbed my stomach. It was jumping like I'd swallowed a chipmunk that was trying to climb its way out. I pulled the van over to the shoulder, sucking in breath as pain spread across my chest.

I dialed my wife on my cell phone as I fumbled with the lever to lean the seat back. I tried to relax in the reclined seat, which allowed more room for my 260-pound body.

"Annie, something's wrong. I'm near Exit 224 in Tennessee in the van, pulled over on the shoulder. My chest is killing me."

I let my arm fall to my side, hanging up the phone.

When Annie and her dad arrived a few hours later, I'd passed out. They got me to the ER in Greenville, where my blood alcohol content tested four times the legal limit. Doctors said my pancreas and gall bladder were trying to shut down, and I was in the beginning stages of cirrhosis. I was drinking myself to death.

It was time to stop.

Without alcohol, I developed a serious case of the shakes. If I tried to eat peas, I slung them everywhere. I jammed my toothbrush into my gums trying to brush my teeth. We had a good laugh about it, and I enjoyed connecting with my family without the numbing wall of alcohol between us. I sat at the table with them at dinner. I played catch with my sons instead of lying listlessly on the couch. I even went to church some and played guitar with the praise band. I was plugging myself back into life, and it felt good.

The lure of the drink, however, is strong, and four months later, my respite was over. I was secretly drinking as much as I ever had.

అఅఅ

"You know, I think I'm coming down with the flu." Jack looked at me strangely. He and I both knew I seemed fine.

"Yeah, I just don't think I'm going to make all of the company events this weekend. Can you just drop me off at my hotel? I think I need to get some rest. I'll see you Monday at the meeting."

I usually stayed with my friend Steve in Los Angeles, but he was out of town. I booked a hotel for two weeks while I worked at the Taylor factory and went to company meetings.

FOUND

Instead of going to my room, I shuffled two blocks to the liquor store, a trek that had become a daily habit. Sometimes I got a taxi because it just seemed like a long way, and I was too drunk to walk. To minimize my trips, I bought liquor by the gallon.

Truly, I desperately wanted to stop drinking. I didn't want to disappoint Annie or my kids anymore. I longed to really *feel* life, to live in the world and feel comfortable there without a mind-altering substance coursing through my system.

My addiction won, though. With a tip of the gallon jug, I surrendered.

࿋ ࿋ ࿋

"There he is!"

The big window in my ground-floor motel room shattered, and men climbed into my room. They carried me out. Lights flashed. Someone punched me in the chest, trying to shock the life back into me.

"Stay with me, man." A guy with dark hair leaned over me. "Come on, talk to me. Do you remember how much you drank? How are you feeling?"

I could barely focus. Didn't he get it? I didn't want to talk. I didn't want to breathe. I was supposed to be asleep forever.

Tubes and wires were stuck all over me. I was freezing and couldn't stop shaking under a pile of blankets.

Why am I here? I just want to go back to sleep. Sleep.

The nurse touched my shoulder. "It's okay. You're in the ICU. You're going to be okay, all right?"

The television in my hospital room was on for hours, only interrupted by the staff psychologist.

"You consumed a lot of alcohol this weekend. Were you trying to kill yourself?"

"No."

"You could have called someone to help you. Is that how you feel? Like no one could help you?"

"No. Look, I was drunk. Just drunk. I guess I drank too much and passed out."

If I tell her what she wants to hear, they'll let me out of here. My professional life is over if anyone finds out.

It turns out that I had called Steve during my weekend of drinking, in which I'd consumed 14 gallons of alcohol. I'd told him I wanted it to be over. When a knock came on the hospital room door, I figured it was him telling me I was fired.

Instead, Stodderd walked in, a guy I'd met a few times at work. *Why in the world was he here?* I knew him, but not really.

"Hey, man." I didn't know what else to say.

"Steve called and said I should come see you."

"Okay?"

Stodderd settled into a chair next to my hospital bed and started talking about his life. He was younger than me, but we'd fought the same battle with alcohol. He described his struggle, his experiences and his victory over the booze.

FOUND

He didn't ask me questions or expect me to comment. I lay on my bed and listened, locked into his story because it was so much like mine. My whole life I'd felt like I was wandering through a foreign country, and finally someone spoke my native language. When Stodderd finished his story, I told him mine. And he listened until I was finished.

Then, I just wanted to go home. I wanted to see Annie. I needed to go to rehab.

After convincing the psychologist to let me go, Stodderd dropped me off at my motel room. The window was boarded up, and when Stodderd opened the door, I almost fell over backward from the smell of alcohol and vomit that smacked me in the face.

The room looked like a war zone, strewn with empty liquor bottles. *How much did I drink this weekend? How many of these gallon bottles have I drunk in my life?*

I talked to God as I dropped the bottles into a garbage bag. I'd already apologized to the motel staff and promised them I'd clean it up the best I could.

I'm broken, God. I don't know where I'm going from here, but I'm not doing this anymore.

I straggled into the airport the next day, exhausted from a sleepless night in the rank motel room and still sick from the alcohol. I shook and sweated bullets through the flight home, worried that my body would betray me before I could get to a bathroom. When I got off the plane in Atlanta, my favorite guitar hadn't made it. For once, I didn't care. Annie picked me up and gave me my schedule for the residential rehab center I'd be going to. I didn't fight her.

ॐॐॐ

The Christian rehab center was full of people like me. Just like Stodderd, we spoke each other's language. The staff told us if we were there to get better for someone else, we would fail. We had to heal for *ourselves.*

"You get right with God, and everything will fall into place," they told us. "Read your Bible. Get to know him."

I had time to read at rehab. The Bible stories I'd first heard from my grandmother came alive again. I remembered the feeling that night I'd listened to the televangelist at 2 a.m. I'd felt like God was with me, and everything was all right. But so much had happened since then. I'd tried to end my life twice, and I hadn't succeeded.

It took some time, but I began to understand that if God didn't have a plan for my life, I wouldn't still be here. I had done a lot of bad, but God had forgiven me for the things I'd done wrong and offered me a new life ahead, free of the past.

When I completed rehab, I walked out with my heart full from what I had learned about God. It was time to start building my life anew — this time, with God in control.

ॐॐॐ

As I got to know God, I got to know myself.

Soon after my return from rehab, I started seeing a counselor.

"Ian," he said. "You're not a mistake. God made you the way you are for a reason."

I don't know why God thinks so much of me, I thought. *But I'm glad he saved me from the grave.*

Through my counselor, I learned I had ADD, which played a part in why I so often felt overwhelmed. I started to work through my fears and anxieties, resting in the fact that God loved me deeply and that no matter what happened he would take care of my family and me.

Most importantly, I stopped hating myself.

"Ian, are you greater than God?" my counselor asked.

"No, not by any stretch."

"It says in the Bible that God removes your sins from you as far as the East is from the West. When he forgives you, it's forgotten, and there's no record of that sin.

"If God can forgive you, why can't you forgive yourself?"

He's right. I'm not greater than God. Who do I think I am?

The hole in my heart once filled so easily with depression and shame now filled with joy. Emotions came and went, but I faced life with a new peace that the God who loved me was in control.

෨෨෨

At the end of a recording session with a few buddies, we started discussing bringing in some more musicians.

"We ought to bring Rob in to play the saxophone sometime," the drummer piped up.

"I don't know," Lee, another musician friend, replied. "He's getting ready to start a church."

"Oh, really?" This caught my interest. Annie and I were looking for a church. "Where's the church going to be?"

"Travelers Rest. They're going to open the doors in October."

The words came out before I could think.

"Do they need a guitar player?"

"Yeah, they do!" Lee had a huge smile on his face.

Do it, I felt like God was speaking to me.

Lee went with me to meet Rob, and soon we were going over set lists and rehearsing for the opening service of Upcountry Church.

When I strummed my guitar for the first set, I knew that I was not just playing music. I was praising God with my heart, my very being. I'd had to relearn how to play the guitar after rehab, as my muscles only knew how to work when they relaxed from alcohol.

I reveled in how God changed my life once I decided to give him control. I'd settled into my thriving guitar repair business in Greenville. I engaged with Annie and my kids, no longer spending my free time passed out on the couch or anxious about sneaking my next drink.

Whether strumming in my studio or playing in the

FOUND

church band, my guitar became a channel connecting me to God. I pray and play, sometimes so full of joy that I cry.

I've played on bigger stages. I've played for thousands of screaming people. I've tasted what it's like to be a rock star.

On stage in church, however, I play for God, and I'm convinced he's the only audience that matters.

LOVED
The Story of Miranda
Written by Angela Welch Prusia

"Hurry!" Sabrina gave a backward glance at the adults lounging around our cluster of RVs. "They won't see us sneak away."

Laughter mixed with the slight breeze. My bike leaned against a pine tree where I left it to join my older cousins.

Sabrina led us away from the campsite. "They won't even notice we're gone."

I trailed after the group, glad they didn't push me aside as the youngest. Excitement spurred me forward.

We stopped in a tall grassy area across from the bait shop. Sabrina pulled out a pack of smokes and lit a cigarette. The smoke curled upward like the mystery clouding her. Sabrina lived with my aunt and uncle and their kids. Beyond the fact that she was in foster care, we knew nothing about her past.

Sabrina flicked her lighter. The flame wavered in the air, the reflection dancing in her dark pupils.

"Any takers?" She exhaled a puff and handed the cigarette to my cousin, who took a drag. I studied the way he inhaled the smoke, taking mental notes so I would look just as cool.

When Sabrina handed me the cigarette, my hands trembled slightly. The bittersweet smell of tobacco burned my nostrils, but I refused to cough. I touched my lips to the white roll, imitating the others. Nicotine filled my lungs, pulling me into its addictive grasp.

I was hooked at age 8.

ৡৡৡৡ

As soon as we returned home from camping, I grabbed my allowance and took off for the store to buy my first box of cigarettes.

The clerk didn't ask questions. The industry didn't have regulations like today.

My parents didn't know.

Not that they cared.

When Daddy wasn't working the swing shift down at the shipyards in Bremerton, Washington, he was meditating in his room. He tried to feed us kids the herbs he believed cleared the mind for deeper meditation, but we refused. Incense often drifted from under his bedroom door, along with the sounds of odd chanting music.

Mom stayed home, but she didn't cook or clean or pay attention to us five kids. We were expected to get ourselves up and off to school. Her only affection went to her sister or her studies. Mom had more degrees than I could count. The few times I saw her and Daddy together, they fought.

I'd disappear to my best friend Lily's house for days without one call from home. I loved hanging out with her family where I got hugs and three meals a day. At our house, food was always an issue. Mom locked food away for herself, but many nights, the grumble of my stomach kept me tossing and turning. Lily's family took me to church sometimes, and I liked the friendly people.

Lily moved schools when her mom got a teaching job at another elementary, and my heart broke. When the other kids picked on me, I became a loner.

In sixth grade, my parents agreed to sign paperwork letting me attend Lily's school. But Lily's popularity fueled my jealousy. If I couldn't be her best friend, no one else would, either. I spread ugly rumors, convincing the rest of the girls that Lily wasn't worth liking.

My plan succeeded, but seeing Lily crying alone in the cafeteria day after day made me feel awful.

"I'm sorry," I finally apologized to her.

Lily accepted my offer but remained guarded around me. I felt even lonelier.

I spent hours by myself playing house in the woods behind our farmhouse. When I got hungry, I ate wild blackberries or apples from the orchard. I set up old dishes I found in the barn from my parents' failed ice cream business and pretended by myself, but I was starved for friends.

Sometimes my brother Darren let me tag along with him when he chopped down trees to build forts in the woods. When I saw him smoking pot with friends, I paid him to get me some. Not long after, Darren introduced me to Skeeter, the sister of his friends Toby and Johnny. We spent our summer days dropping acid and smoking pot in the converted garage which served as a bedroom for the boys. The ceiling turned into a canvas for my hallucinations — floating mermaids and vivid colored sparklers. Drugs became my connection to make friends.

বৈৰৈৰ

A few days before my 12th birthday, I flirted with one of Toby's 19-year-old friends while we got high at a party. I rubbed his back while we talked, and soon he pulled me into a camper on the property. There I lost my virginity.

His attention made me crave more. Anyone who glanced my way got me into bed.

When one of the boys moved to Pennsylvania, I hopped on a bus across the country to surprise him.

"What're you doing here?" Geno squeaked over the phone.

I played with the cord on the pay phone and looked around the bus stop. My stomach grumbled. "Surprise," I muttered into the phone. "Can you come get me?"

I took a seat in a corner while I waited.

"Hey, sweet thang." An older man approached me. Crooked teeth showed when his lips spread into a creepy grin. "You hungry?"

Fear made my skin crawl. I clutched my bag.

"I can get you some nice new clothes." He took a seat beside me, and the stench made my eyes water.

A cop approached. "Is he bothering you, miss?"

I breathed a sigh of relief. "I'm waiting for my boyfriend."

The guy disappeared into the shadows, while the police officer consulted his notes. "We got a missing person's report with your description."

I didn't attempt to lie while he made a few phone calls. My parents wouldn't miss my absence, so I figured Geno must've called the police.

"You'll spend the night in emergency placement," the cop explained.

My hands trembled from lack of nicotine. "I need a smoke."

A caseworker soon arrived and called my parents. She bought me a pack of cigarettes and took me to a foster home for the night.

I boarded a nonstop flight the next day without ever seeing Geno.

శీశీశీ

Six months later, my parents angered me enough to run away again. This time, I left with Kimmy, one of my brother's friends.

"Drop your bag." She called up to me from below my bedroom window. I tossed it into her arms and hurried down the stairs.

We bummed our first ride on the outside of town. It wasn't hard with our provocative clothes. We looked older than 16 and 12.

"Where you ladies headed?" The guy undressed us with his eyes.

"California." Kimmy gave him a coy smile.

I leaned back against the man's passenger seat and let the music carry me away. I didn't care where we landed as long as we escaped.

Our first night we spent drinking and dropping acid with two soldiers at Fort Lewis, Washington. Kimmy slept with one of the guys, while I cruised around the base with the other soldier.

The next day a family drove us to Oregon and dropped us off at a truck stop. An older trucker named Grizzly picked us up before he found another safe trucker headed south. Before we parted, he kissed me. I didn't have the heart to tell him I saw him like a father — not a boyfriend.

"Take good care of these two," he told his friend as we pulled out of the truck stop.

Our trip took 10 days and cost us less than $20. We charmed a handful of truck drivers who gave us rides and food. Somewhere along the route, Kimmy convinced me to change our destination to Arizona where her older sister lived with relatives because she was too wild for her parents.

The last trucker drove us straight to the house. But after a week, Kimmy's aunt convinced me to call my parents, and our fun together ended. My parents made arrangements for me to stay with my uncle and his girlfriend who lived nearby until they could buy a plane ticket.

Uncle Harry lived in a trashy trailer. He fed me once a day while I slept the hours away on the couch and partied with the neighborhood kids at night. I had to shave my head when I got lice and made a visit to the doctor to treat an STD.

I turned 13 while I stayed with my uncle. For kicks, a bunch of us broke into the high school and rode around on some golf carts we discovered. The night ended with a trip to the hospital when one of the kids cut his eye on Plexiglas.

A few days later, two plane tickets arrived in the mail. Uncle Harry would escort me home.

❧❧❧

Still a loner at school, I couldn't handle seeing all the girls laughing and having fun together. I'd disappear into the bathroom to punch the wall in frustration. I didn't know what to do to gain their acceptance.

Miserable, I dropped out of school in eighth grade at age 13 and moved in with my new boyfriend, Kyle, and his grandparents who thought I was 17. I met Kyle while smoking pot. Since he was the only guy who waited to sleep with me until we'd been dating for three months, I was convinced he loved me. My inexperience blinded me to his calculative behavior and desire for control.

"You can't eat that." Kyle grabbed a jar of mayonnaise out of my hand shortly after we moved in together. "That's fattening."

His anger surprised me. I weighed less than 100 pounds, but I did what he demanded since I didn't want to get overweight like my mother. When his next outburst drew blood, I wiped off my face and tried not to cry.

Kyle's control tightened. We moved into a trailer a few feet from my parents' house, but he limited my time with them. The trailer didn't have plumbing, so I cooked our meals at their house. Often, Kyle forced me to get down on my knees and serve him the meals I prepared. He wouldn't let me use the bathroom at my parents and pushed me to steal from them. Daddy had to know I was taking quarters from his stash in his work boots, but he never said anything. He and my mom mostly seemed glad Kyle kept me from running. They never intervened, even when they heard my screams of pain through the paper-thin walls.

Whenever I questioned Kyle, he made me beg for forgiveness, earning it by agreeing to do whatever he wanted. I hated meth because it deprived me of sleep, but Kyle forced me to take the drug so we could have sex for days. In jealous rages, he beat me until I confessed to infidelity, though I had always remained faithful to him. *How could I sleep with anyone when he has such an iron grip on my life?* Each passing year, Kyle's hold on me got stronger. I dropped to 75 pounds, believing his lies that I deserved his regular beatings.

Kyle worshipped the Devil and filled our home with satanic paraphernalia — black candles, a skull and books about magic and death. Kyle donned a black mask and took me to the place where he performed his rituals. We walked two miles along the highway at night toward the clearing on his grandparents' property where he would build a fire. He called on demons, while he chanted around rising flames. The force of power drew me, and I didn't resist when Kyle cut my arm with a knife and pledged me to the Devil.

Not long before I turned 17, I stared into the bathroom mirror. Dead eyes stared back. I hardly recognized the shell of the girl in the glass. *How had I become this person?*

I longed for my freedom.

Despite how mean I'd been, Lily called every year on my birthday. When I invited her to the trailer, she got uncomfortable with Kyle and confided her feelings to me. I'd convinced myself that he was good for me for so long, her perspective jolted my thinking.

The next time Kyle beat me, I fought back for the first time. Emotion surged through me, and I grabbed a knife. I wanted to kill him, but I couldn't. He got the upper hand and kicked me until I curled into a little ball on the floor. My body finally went numb, but I could barely move for days.

I began to plan my escape. I admitted sleeping with our meth friends, knowing Kyle's jealousy would work in my favor. He broke our ties with meth, and I got clean.

Kyle saw my restlessness and didn't want to lose me. He knew my desire for a child, so he tried to appease me.

"Can I take dance lessons with Lily?" I begged him when I didn't get pregnant.

I couldn't believe it when he agreed. My parents paid

for ballet shoes and several months of lessons. I could practically taste my freedom. Dance would be my ticket to escape.

After a couple lessons, Kyle began to suspect something. I seduced him to distract him from questioning me. I wanted to take more clothes, but I couldn't risk his suspicions. I grabbed a folder of poetry I'd written before my years with Kyle and left for dance. Other than the jeans and T-shirt I wore over my leotard, my dance shoes were the only other possession I carried in a small backpack.

"I have to quit dance lessons," I explained to the instructor as soon as I made it to class.

"Is everything okay?" Her surprise turned to concern when she saw the tears well in my eyes.

"I need to escape," I confessed. "My boyfriend is abusing me."

She agreed to refund me the balance of nearly $300 and wished me luck.

Money in hand, I headed for the foot ferry at the pier.

Terror seized me. I froze in the middle of a current of people getting off the ferry. The faces of strangers blurred around me.

What was I thinking? I was all alone. Kyle would find me and kill me.

Someone bumped me, jostling me out of my paralysis. I hurried to the nearest pay phone and punched in Lily's number with a shaky hand.

Come on. Pick up.

"Hello?" The familiar voice brought a flood of emotions. A lump lodged in my throat, blocking my words. "Hello?"

"Lily?" I managed to blurt out.

"Miranda?" Her concern came through the line and wrapped me in love. I wasn't alone.

"I left Kyle." The words sounded so strange on my lips. "Can I stay with you a few days?"

Lily picked me up 30 minutes later. I collapsed into the passenger seat an emotional wreck, never so grateful for her friendship in my entire life.

❧❧❧

I stayed with Lily until her roommates got uncomfortable with me hanging out. Pot no longer appealed to me after a bad drug trip, so I quit. For the next several months, I bounced from home to home, staying with my brother, a boyfriend, an uncle and finally — my new fiancé.

A month after my wedding by a justice of the peace, Jeremy cheated on me, so I left him, but stayed in Connecticut where he was stationed with the Navy. I finished my GED through a military program and got my first full-time job working at a child care center. A year later, I decided to return home to begin college classes.

When Lily found out I was back in town, we started hanging out, and she invited me to church. The message there was simple, yet profound.

"For God so loved the world that he gave his one and only son, that whoever believes in him shall not perish but have everlasting life."

I remembered memorizing John 3:16 as a kid at her church, but now the meaning was clear.

God loved me. He sent his son to die for me. He was willing to forgive me of all my mess-ups. He was about to heal all the broken parts of my heart. I'd been so starved for love, I reveled in this new understanding.

The pastor concluded by asking if anyone wanted prayer. Tears sprang to my eyes. I walked forward with Lily and fell to the floor, as if kneeling at the foot of the cross.

"Jesus," I said, sniffling, "can you please forgive me for the way I've lived my life?"

Immediately, peace and joy washed over me like a tender kiss from my Savior. I'd never felt safer. I had hope for the first time in my life. My bondage to the Devil was severed. I was now a child of God.

I realized then that God was with me. He'd always been with me. I was never as alone as I thought.

"This is for you." I took off my ring of pink roses made from Black Hills gold and handed it to Lily. It was a small token of my gratitude. She'd saved my life by introducing me to Jesus. I wanted to give her a gift.

Tears trickled down Lily's cheek. She placed the ring on her finger and gave me an opal ringed in diamonds. I learned that her parents had tried to adopt me as a child, but my parents' unwillingness prevented me from joining their family. Knowing that Lily's parents loved me added to my joy.

Three days later on Independence Day, Lily invited me to go kayaking with friends in the Puget Sound. As we paddled toward Blake Island, we talked about Jesus and my newfound faith.

"Do you want to be baptized as a symbol of your new life?"

When I agreed, she baptized me in the water as soon as we landed.

As the cold water washed over me, I knew everything was going to be okay. Jesus bought my freedom. My old life was gone.

࿇࿇࿇

I'd been smoking cigarettes since I was 8 years old, and I knew it was a bad habit. When I asked Jesus to come into my life, I felt like he gave me the strength to shake off nicotine's hold on me. I quit smoking cigarettes.

Church became my new home. I took notes, studied the Bible and began to pray. A new respect for myself welled up inside, and I saw it reflected in the way others treated me as well. I belonged to God. New purpose breathed life into my days.

An opportunity opened up to go to Italy as a missionary, so I asked God whether he wanted me to go or not. When it felt like the answer became obvious, I sold everything. Someone at church bought me a plane ticket, so I flew to Rome where I taught kindergarten for a church school and grew in my faith. I studied the Bible during my spare time and wrote poetry again. But this time, my words weren't filled with sorrow. My poems were praises to Jesus, who saved me.

> *My Father, I honor you.*
> *Praises be to the one who forgot my sin.*
> *God saved me from a life of pain and hopelessness.*
> *Oh, how long were the years without you, Lord,*
> *I did not call for help.*
> *You never abandoned me in my foolishness.*
> *You watched over me, Lord.*
> *Be glorified in my life that others may feel your joy.*
> *Although the evil one had me in his house*
> *And I longed to eat at his table,*
> *You, gracious God, did not hold my sins against me.*
> *For, Lord, I cried out to you in my pain*
> *And you rescued me.*

A year later, I joined the Army as a chaplain's assistant. In addition to writing a daily email morning devotion, I loved being able to counsel soldiers.

Another assistant chaplain asked me to marry him, and though we stayed together for eight years, he seemed committed more to the business side of being a chaplain than to connecting with Jesus. I stopped writing and began to neglect my daily time reading the Bible and talking with Jesus. My heart grew cold as I fell away from God.

We divorced, and I returned to the party lifestyle. Guilt plagued me for failing my marriage and failing God.

A year later, I met Randy, and his love for his daughters touched my heart. We moved to South Carolina for his job and gained custody of his three girls soon after our wedding. My heart soared. I'd always wanted to be a mother.

༒༒༒

Making lunches for the girls and kissing their bruised knees filled an ache inside me.

But something was still missing.

I tried going to church. But I never reconnected with God, so a Sunday service here and there left me empty.

When Anna, my oldest stepdaughter, was invited by a friend to visit Upcountry Church, we joined her. Walking into the sanctuary, it felt like God saying, *Welcome home. I've missed you.*

A few weeks later, Pastor Rob preached from Genesis, and my heart cracked open. I didn't realize how far I'd drifted from Jesus. I fell to my knees at the altar. I ached from missing the relationship we'd shared.

"Forgive me," I begged God. Tears streamed down my face. "I'm so sorry for screwing up again. Forgive me for letting the temporary pleasures of this world creep into my life and take your place. I need you, Jesus. I've missed you so much."

His peace was waiting for me.

FOUND

༒༒༒

The people at Upcountry Church have become family, especially since my own biological ties remain rocky. After five years in South Carolina, this is the first time we truly feel at home.

For my husband, a new believer, Pastor Rob's messages are easy to understand and practical enough to use in daily life. The girls love the programs for children and youth. During our car rides home from church, they get excited telling us everything they've learned.

Recently, Anna returned home from a retreat to Myrtle Beach with the youth group.

"I feel closer to God," she confided to me.

I couldn't stop smiling, knowing she's embraced what took me years to discover. Unconditional love was a foreign concept to me with my history of being ignored, controlled or beaten. But once I surrendered to Jesus, I saw evidence of his tender love all around me — in my friendship with Lily, in my husband, Randy, who loves me despite my past, and in my three sweet girls.

My mistakes don't change his love. God still loves me. As he says in Isaiah 54, "Though the mountains be shaken and the hills be removed, yet my unfailing love for you will not be shaken … no weapon forged against you will prevail."

God loves me.

He really loves me.

I'm not alone. I'm loved.

THE ROAD TO RICHES
The Story of Abby and Carson
Written by Lisa Bradshaw

Abby

I stood over the toilet in my friend's bathroom, nervous about making myself throw up for the first time.

"Come on, Abby. Just bend over and do it," Jennifer told me. "It doesn't hurt."

I wanted to get thin and stay thin. Throwing up after eating worked for Jennifer.

Still, I hesitated.

"It doesn't hurt?"

"Not a bit."

I pressed the tip of my fingers against the back of my throat and gagged.

કે કે કે

My mom and dad loved my brother and me. We had a good family life. Even so, at 14, I felt insecure, inadequate and unworthy.

Then I met Jennifer.

I had issues, and she seemed to have answers. We quickly became friends.

Jennifer introduced me to drugs and alcohol and showed me how she lost weight and kept it off. I tried it all, wanting to cover up the way I felt about myself.

FOUND

I began throwing up with more frequency, convinced it was the answer to improving my self-image. I could eat what I wanted and never gain an ounce of weight as long as I threw up before my body absorbed the unwanted calories.

I didn't think my parents noticed what I was doing until my mom confronted me after she found small trash bags of dried vomit tied up tightly and hidden in the back of my closet.

"Abby, what is happening to you?"

"I haven't done it in a while," I lied. "I just forgot to throw them out."

"Well, this better stop, or we're taking you to the doctor."

It did not stop. I just tried hiding it better.

One morning, when I thought everyone else had left the house, I went into the bathroom after breakfast to throw up. My dad stood outside the bathroom door waiting for me when I came out.

"I don't ever want to catch you doing that again!" he yelled.

Behind his anger, I saw his sadness. He felt helpless against the agony my bulimia brought to our family, just as I did.

My mom kept her word and took me to the doctor, but I only gave the doctor a modified version of what I had been doing, how often I was doing it and how long it had been going on. The doctor suggested I enter treatment.

"I can stop on my own," I assured him and my parents. "I know I can."

I think my parents wanted to believe me, just as I wanted to believe myself, but they did not realize I was making myself throw up every day and after every meal.

For the rest of that day after seeing the doctor, I tried not to throw up. After dinner, I went to my room and paced, trying to distract myself from walking into the bathroom and getting rid of the calories I'd consumed during dinner. But by then, it felt unnatural to eat and not throw up. My mind raced as I imagined how I would look in the morning.

Will my stomach be less flat?

Will my pants feel tight?

Will people at school notice I was just slightly larger than the day before?

I managed to control myself until my parents went to bed. I knew I had better find a way to throw up where they could not hear me and to hide the evidence where they wouldn't find it.

I snuck downstairs and out the back door to a trash can near the garage door. I brought a small bag with me and threw up in the bag, then tied it shut and shoved it under the rest of the trash before slipping back inside unnoticed.

By then, I did not even need to use my fingers to force myself to throw up. Just bending over was my body's cue to eliminate whatever nutrition my mother had provided for me for breakfast, lunch or dinner. My knuckles no longer bore bite marks from shoving my fingers down my throat. And if my face looked weary, I just covered up the dark circles under my eyes with makeup. At school, I just had to make sure no one else was in the girls' restroom when I did it. At home, I used the outside trash can, as I had the first night after going to the doctor. Sometimes I threw up in the yard and covered it with dirt or hosed the vomit off the grass when no one was looking. Finding new and creative ways of throwing up without getting caught became my distraction from dealing with why I was throwing up in the first place. And if my parents were on to me, they didn't show it.

࿔࿔࿔

Carson

It was the night before Thanksgiving. We heard a knock at the door but weren't expecting anyone.

"I'll get it." I jumped up from the floor where I'd been playing a game with my three brothers.

"Hold up, Carson." My father followed behind me. At just 6 years old, I was too young to answer the door alone in the evening.

Standing on our front porch were a man and a woman from our church. One of them was holding a basket full of food, including a huge turkey.

"Sir, our congregation would like you to have this basket of blessings," he politely said as he handed my father the basket.

"Yes, we pray you and your family will enjoy the blessings of the season," the woman said softly as she stroked my hair and patted me on the head.

I looked at my father with excitement.

"Oh, boy!" I cheered. "Look at all this food. Is it all for us?"

"It sure is. We hope you enjoy it," the man answered.

I looked at my father, expecting him to be excited, too.

"Um, well, thank you," my father said, clearing his throat and unable to make eye contact with the couple.

"You're welcome, sir."

"Yes, you're so very welcome."

My father slowly closed the door, then placed the basket on the kitchen table. My mom and my brothers and I rummaged through the entire basket cheerfully calling out each product inside it.

"Look, Mom," I shouted. "Look at all the bread rolls."

"And there's cranberry sauce," my oldest brother exclaimed, licking his lips in anticipation of our feast for the next day.

"And a pumpkin pie," my older brother chimed in. "I love pumpkin pie."

"It was very kind of them to think of us, wasn't it, Jim?" my mom said to my father. She was determined to make receiving the gift from church fun for us. My dad's face said it all. It grieved him to know he could not provide for his family, despite how hard he worked. It bothered him even more that others regarded us as needy.

"Yes, it was," he answered quietly. He was grateful but

humiliated. He walked out of the kitchen and into their bedroom, then shut the door. He did not come out the rest of the night.

ॐॐॐ

Abby

By the time I graduated, I still hadn't managed to shake bulimia's hold on me.

It felt good, in the moment. Later, it only left me feeling worse.

Would I ever find a way out? It seemed impossible.

ॐॐॐ

Carson

The primary thing I learned from growing up poor in a predominantly affluent city was that I wanted to be rich. I did not just want to avoid poverty, I wanted to have more money than anyone I'd ever known and more possessions than I could even imagine.

In high school, I got tired of seeing my friends roll up to school in their bright and shiny new sports cars, gifts from their parents.

"Hey, man. Check it out."

"Yeah, cool," I responded, trying not to seem jealous.

"Wanna go for a spin?"

"Sure, why not?"

As I climbed inside and smelled the new car smell for the first time in my life, I was instantly dizzied by the determination that I would one day drive a car just like it. As we raced down neighborhood streets with the stereo blasting and people looking at us as we passed by, I got hooked on the thrill of it all.

Perhaps my longing for money and material things would not have been so consuming had it not been for my humble surroundings compared to my friends' lavish lifestyles. Rather than teaching me humility, it only made me want what they had — money became everything to me.

By the time I left home, my parents no longer lived below the poverty level, but they could never compete with the money thrown around by my friends and their parents. When I left, I vowed never to be like them. Being poor was not an option.

ॐॐॐ

Abby

Carson was different than the other guys I'd dated. He seemed more put together. He drove a nice car and was always polite. It wasn't long before the two of us began dating exclusively.

Within a year of our first date, we got engaged. He thought I was the perfect girl for him, and I did my best to maintain that image for him during our engagement and even after we married, never telling him of my alcohol abuse or bulimia.

We both drank socially, which made it easier to satisfy

my desire for alcohol without drawing attention to it. The bulimia proved more difficult to hide, just as it had been as a teenager when I lived in my parents' home.

I knew how to hide it, but now it was different. I wasn't hiding it from my prying parents who I wanted to stay out of my business and leave me alone. I was hiding it from my husband who was supposed to be able to trust me. I could not bear the thought of telling him the truth, but I kept doing it. Only when I got pregnant with our first child did I manage to stop until he was 3 months old. I felt relief I could make it that long and falsely believed it meant I was getting better.

I settled into motherhood and thought I had my issues under control. I focused on my son and what he needed but grew increasingly dissatisfied with my marriage. I'd hoped that with the birth of our child, Carson would focus more on our family and less on his work.

"Can you just stay home and be with us today?" I asked Carson many different times, but I always heard the same response.

"There isn't time for that. You know I have been working on this deal for a while. Once it closes, we'll be set. Then I can focus more on our family."

I'd hoped becoming a father would prompt Carson to spend more time with us, satisfied with the life we had built. It did the opposite. He worked more and spent less time at home. He believed he was doing the right thing for all of us, but I felt alone, and the only way I knew to deal with my feelings was to mask them — and throw up.

THE ROAD TO RICHES

૰૰૰

Carson

My obsession with earning money continued. We had an adequate home and the material possessions to go along with it, but it didn't seem to be enough. Becoming a father only made me work harder to provide what my own father could not provide his family.

When I would come home from work and Abby seemed distant or disinterested in me, I felt sure that I was not good enough.

"Hi, honey. How was your day?" I would ask her. Abby would be trying to settle the baby and serve dinner at the same time.

"Fine. It was fine," she would snap at me. "Here, can you take him? My hands are full."

Then we would eat dinner in silence, and I would retreat to our bedroom for the night.

I worked harder and earned more money, but that only widened the distance between Abby and me. We were growing further apart in our marriage, not only because of the long hours I spent at work, but because I never fully engaged in our family life. I was so preoccupied with wanting more, I didn't enjoy what was already before me — a loving wife and child.

From the outside looking in, we were the perfect family. I was successful and made a lot of money. We attended church, we had friends and we owned a beautiful home. I made sure my family wanted for nothing. I would do anything to keep my dream alive to be rich, not realizing how much it would cost my family.

༄༄༄

Abby

Soon, I was pregnant with our second child, and my bulimia was out of control. The more stress I felt in our marriage, the more violent and frequent my bulimic episodes became.

I struggled with it, worried I was hurting my unborn baby. I would overeat, purge and then eat a normal meal. I knew what I was doing wasn't healthy, but I tried hard to make sure my daughter was getting what she needed.

After our daughter was born, I went back to throwing up every single day.

It wasn't long before Carson decided to sell his business. By then, he was traveling for speaking engagements, teaching business development and making real estate investments.

Soon, we packed up and moved to Indiana for three months for one of Carson's business opportunities. I did not want to go. We had just started going to the church Carson's oldest brother, Michael's, family attended, and I felt at home there. I'd attended church occasionally growing up and had gone to Christian school as a child, but I never really understood what it meant to have a relationship with God outside of the obligation of church. At Michael's church, I attended Bible study, made new friends and started to feel closer to God and understand what that relationship could mean for my life. I did not want to continue on the way I was living. I was searching for peace and understanding. I was searching for God, and church no longer felt like an obligation to me. I enjoyed going and actually got something out of it for the first time in my life.

"I don't want to go," I told Carson.

"We have to go. It's a great opportunity for me. For us," he said, trying to convince me that what awaited us in Indiana would be better than what we had in California.

I did not have the courage to confront him anymore. I knew he was just chasing more money and taking our children and me along for the ride. No matter what I said to assure him that we had more than enough, he would not hear it.

"I'm setting up our financial future," he justified. "I'm doing all of this for us."

"Okay, you're right," I told Carson. I did not think he was right, but there was no reasoning with him.

We went to Indiana, only to return within three months. Then we went back to Indiana again a few months later. It was a constant chase after a dream that would never be satisfied, and I tired of trying to keep up.

We both suffered in the silence that had taken over our marriage. I did not feel like Carson was taking care of our family or me, and I pulled away from him more and more.

"What is wrong with you? I'm working so hard for us, and you don't appreciate it," Carson said to me.

FOUND

"I don't know what's wrong. I don't know," I answered in tears.

This was the ongoing dialogue in our home. It was constant and unrelenting. I felt sad and tired and lonely. While Carson built our financial future, the walls between us grew taller and stronger.

ๆๆๆ

Carson

Nothing I did satisfied my wife. Abby pulled further and further away from me, and I felt more and more rejected. We lacked intimacy, we lacked communication and we didn't believe anything could make it better.

During that time, my father flew to Indiana to help me drive our car home to California. On the drive back from Indiana, the car broke down.

While we waited for a tow truck, my father texted someone.

"What are you doing, Dad?"

"Oh, it's an old friend from the Navy. It'll only take a minute."

Then, he excused himself to sit inside the car and talk privately.

I had a feeling it was not a buddy from the Navy. He texted with delight and seemed invigorated by the exchange.

A week after we got home, my mom called me crying hysterically.

"He's leaving me!" she cried, literally gasping for breath.

"What are you talking about? Who's leaving you?" I asked, completely caught off guard by her phone call and her frantic voice.

"He looked up his high school sweetheart on his way back from Indiana and found her on Facebook. He went to see her on his way home."

"He what?"

I could not believe what my mom was telling me. My parents were approaching their 40th wedding anniversary.

My father took a detour on his way home in my vehicle to go see his old girlfriend, and now he is leaving my mom for her after 40 years of marriage? It doesn't make sense. My father has always been a family man and a godly man. He quotes scripture and raised us in church. How can this be true?

"He said all these years were a mistake, and he is going to leave and be with her."

At this point, I was a man in my early 30s with a wife and kids of my own. I knew I'd taken them for granted and deceived myself into thinking everything was okay. Witnessing my father's rash behavior suddenly made me realize I, too, was headed down a dangerous path.

"Mom, I'm so sorry. I'm so sorry."

I had no more words to offer her at that point. Part of me blamed myself for having him help me drive back from Indiana.

Another part of me knew from regretting my own

behavior in my marriage that he had no one to blame but himself.

I confronted my father.

"I have been miserable my whole marriage. Marrying your mom was all a mistake," he confessed to me.

"Then you're saying your four sons were also a mistake."

He considered leaving years before, he told me. I thought that, if he hadn't left before, perhaps he would change his mind on his own again, or I could convince him to stay.

"Please, Dad. Don't do this," I begged him.

"It's just something I have to do."

My father left my mother for the other woman. In one swift decision within a week of returning from Indiana with me, my father left my mom, and in turn, he left my brothers and me, our wives and our children — he left us all.

There was no making sense of it. It broke my mom to the point that Abby and I invited her to live with us, worrying about her mental state.

My father leaving brought every bit of pain and rejection to the surface in my own life. I feared I was bound in this life to destroy my own son if I continued as I had been living.

I knew something had to change, but I had no idea how to do it. I was not capable of such enormous change on my own.

Soon after my father left, I went on a camping trip

with my family in Northern California when something powerful happened.

I am still not sure if I was awake or asleep, but sometime around 4 a.m., I found myself standing on a dirt road facing two human-like figures. Then I heard a voice.

"These are the demons that have controlled your family for generations," the voice began. "One of these is Idolatry, and the other is Rejection. They have ruled your family for years. Are they going to rule you?"

I looked at the faces of the two figures. Rejection looked satisfied with his work, as if he had won the battle and his reward was my soul.

Idolatry looked arrogant. "I will rule your life forever," he boasted. "You will never free yourself from my grip. Your family will never be free. You will go to your grave with that same empty feeling, still wanting more."

Whether it was a dream or real, I did not know. I felt like I was actually standing on the dirt road in front of the demons that had held me captive all of my life. It was more real than anything I had ever experienced.

The next morning, I made an excuse to leave camp to call my oldest brother.

Michael had a strong faith, and I trusted him not to think I'd gone completely crazy. I knew he would listen to me.

I explained everything to him in detail.

"You know that was not a dream, right?" he calmly asked. "You know that was real, and the Lord just gave you a gift."

"I think so."

"God is showing you where you are in life and where you will continue to go. This is the fork in the road where you can choose to live your way, the way you have been living, or you can choose to live a life with the Lord, which is nothing like the path you are on now."

I grew up in church. I learned about God and knew who he was, but I had never really followed him. I was not sure what to do.

I hung up the phone and drove around, trying to understand what had happened to me. Part of me was mystified. Part of me was angry at the notion that demons controlled me.

I'll show you, God. I'm in control here.

But then I had an overwhelming feeling that this was, in fact, a turning point for me.

If I trust in you, can I be set free?

Can this be a new beginning for me?

Can I become an honorable man deserving of my family's love and devotion?

Can I finally come to know you, God, and change my life with your help?

I spent the next few days contemplating what all of it meant, and when we returned from our camping trip, I went to Michael's house to talk with him again.

"I have been lost. Work has always come before my family," I began, confessing all manner of sins to Michael. "This is where I am right now."

Michael listened as I sobbed. I'd been on my knees

before God at other times in my life, but every time, I'd stood back up the same man.

This time, I knew it was different. This time, I gave it all to God.

"I give it all to you. Whatever you want me to give up, I will give up. Whatever you want me to bring to you, I will bring it to you, God," I prayed with my brother at my side.

When I stood up, I was a changed man. I knew I would never be the same man, nor did I want to be. I felt the desire to be whole in God's eyes and to restore my marriage.

I had confessed things to Michael and asked God's forgiveness. Had I felt like God wanted me to tell Abby about what I had done, I would have told her. I would have told her everything and risked my marriage to do it, but I didn't believe God wanted me to confess those things to her. Looking back, I believe God was letting me handle one thing at a time.

I got up from my knees that day feeling zero guilt. It would not stay that way, but for a time, I stood before God a renewed man with his will for my life before me.

అంఅంఅం

Abby

I confided in Michael's wife, Caroline, about the mess of our lives and the struggles in our marriage. Throughout our discussions, she told me to continue praying for

Carson, but I had not yet dealt with my own problems. I still hid in the bathroom and used food and purging to mask my loneliness, pain and worries.

A few days after our camping trip, Carson told me what God revealed to him. He told me God had shown him his demons of Idolatry and Rejection, and I felt sure the power of God was at work in our lives. For the first time in my life, I began to receive and accept it. Carson had accepted the Lord, and I felt God was beginning to answer my prayers.

Seeing the changes in Carson gave me hope that we could begin again, but I still feared what would happen if I confessed to Carson all I had been hiding from him. The night I told the women at Bible study about my bulimia, they encouraged me to go home and tell Carson the truth.

I felt like I was going to explode if I did not tell him immediately and decided it was time for me to come clean.

"Carson, wake up," I said, turning on the light and rubbing his legs under the covers of our bed.

"What? What's the matter?" Carson asked, as he rubbed his eyes and tried to adjust to the light in the room.

"I have something to tell you. I've been hiding it from you for years." I took a deep breath, silently praying my confession would not end our marriage.

"What is it?"

I started crying uncontrollably, and Carson looked scared.

"I am bulimic. I have been for years, and I have been

hiding it from you. I was even doing it when I was pregnant with Katy."

The words came out of my mouth so fast, I think Carson had a hard time keeping up with what I was saying.

"Did you hear me? I said I am bulimic. I have been lying to you. I have hidden it from you since the day we met."

He sat up in our bed and opened his arms to me.

"Come here," he told me.

I stood still.

"Please come over here," he asked again.

I was stunned. I did not expect him to want to embrace me. I expected him to be angry with me for keeping it from him or to blame me for my part in our unraveling marriage. Instead, he embraced me and showed me love. I fell into his arms and cried tears of relief for having told the truth.

"I'm so ashamed. I could have hurt our daughter," I cried, clutching Carson's body as he held me even tighter.

"But you didn't. She's fine. You're going to be okay. We're going to be okay," he assured me, stroking my hair, then wiping my tears.

A huge weight lifted from my shoulders after telling Carson the truth, but I still did not know how to stop hurting myself. It felt so good to tell him the truth, but I knew that I would be expected to quit and that it wouldn't be easy. *Maybe we can come together and deal with this,* I thought. *At least we're headed in the right direction.*

FOUND

In the weeks afterward, Carson remained supportive. I struggled every day not to do what I had been doing to my body for years. I feared how I would control my weight without throwing up, but I also feared how I would ever gain control of my life if I didn't stop. I chose to attend a prayer meeting at our church. During the meeting, I realized I had two options: I could keep hurting myself and stay on the same path I'd been on for most of my life, or I could quit. I knew I had to decide, but I wasn't sure if I was ready to take the steps I needed to stop purging. I left the meeting feeling worn out by the burdens I carried and unsure of which road to take.

The morning after the prayer meeting, I went into the bathroom still feeling hopeless and threw up again. I began sobbing and praying for God to forgive me for continuing to hurt myself. As I cried to God for help, I saw a vision of myself with a huge iron bondage collar around my neck, being dragged into the bathroom by a chain attached to the collar. The horrific image shocked me. But I believed God showed me the image of bondage so I could break the chains and be set free.

That was the final time I hurt myself by throwing up. I no longer saw myself as a person who had to violently purge to rid myself of what mounted inside me. I saw myself as someone forgiven by God, and that set me free. It was a new beginning.

THE ROAD TO RICHES

❧❧❧

Carson

I knew I needed to step away from the work that kept me away from home. I also needed to stop chasing money and worshipping it. We were in debt, we were in the middle of a lawsuit in business and we were desperate to start fresh, even if it meant we might lose it all. But we had each other, and God was showing me that having each other, with him in the center of our marriage, was all we needed.

I had already decided to walk away from my high-paying job when I overheard a man at church who was a contractor say he needed help with a job he was doing.

"I can help you," I told him.

David looked shocked by my offer and even chuckled at the thought of it.

"I don't think you understand. This is a laboring job, not pencil pushing."

"I know what it is. I'll do it," I continued, firmly believing this was the right thing to do.

"This is just for one day. And it only pays $10 an hour. No more," he cautioned.

I had already turned down other job offers that paid more money, but I felt sure that God wanted me to work with David. "That's not a problem. When do we start?"

David looked at me like I was crazy. He knew about my earning potential and lavish lifestyle. Everyone knew because I had made sure of it.

"You're sure?"

"I'm sure."

"Well, okay, then. I'll pick you up."

The first day I worked for David, he realized I had more experience than he thought. He asked me to help him complete the project and eventually asked me to stay on for a few months.

David and I were complete opposites, but I believe God used him to heal the wounds my father left behind. David had no reason to think twice about me, to ask me how I was doing or to care about me at all. But he did. Every day I went to work, he loved me like a father. He even encouraged me not to put up a front with other people — as I was so often tempted to do. When my father left, I felt rejected and unloved, and I believe God knew I needed to spend time with a good man like David.

I was overwhelmed by everything going on in our lives. Mom had moved in with us after Dad left. Abby had just admitted her struggles with alcohol and bulimia. We were trying to keep up with our house and all our cars. Our possessions were becoming a burden in and of themselves. All the while I tried to convince myself that God would not give me more than I could bear.

When I told David my reasoning, he said, "That's a lie straight from Satan. The Lord will always give you more than you can handle. That's your reminder that you can't rely on your own strength. You have to trust God for everything that you need."

I was dumbfounded. My whole life had been about

controlling my own destiny. Even though Abby and I felt like we were in over our heads, we started to realize we could rely on God to provide for us and carry us through.

During that time, I accepted a few business management consulting contracts, but I stopped traveling for speaking engagements. As I decreased my workload, God increased my marriage — tenfold.

But it was not long before I found myself in my brother Michael's garage seeking advice.

I still had to deal with what had made me chase money in the first place.

The voices from my vision tormented me. The voices of Rejection and Idolatry seemed to mock me. It got so bad that I asked Michael and a church elder to pray over me. *I've had these voices taunting me for too long,* I thought. *I can't take it anymore.*

As they prayed over me, I suddenly felt better. As strange as it sounds, I left my brother's house and spent the next few days in total peace. For the first time in my memory, I could hold a conversation with someone and not rip him or her apart in my head. I came to believe that I had not been the one ripping anyone apart, but the enemy was doing the ripping to keep me isolated from other people and from God.

Keep him at a distance.

Don't let her get close to you.

Reject her, before she rejects you.

Don't trust him, he just wants your money.

It had been months since I asked God into my life, but

this new work with him was just beginning. It took time to face everything God had in store for me. If forced to come to grips with everything at once, I might have been too afraid to move forward. Either way, God's timing was perfect in me, through me and for me.

In this new walk, one thing loomed in the distance — another wrong I had to make right.

࿁࿁࿁

Abby

Carson and I were closer than we had ever been. I had told him about the bulimia, and together, God freed us from the troubles weighing us down. I thought the worst was behind us. No more confessions. No more demons. I thought we were on the other side of what many marriages rarely survive, but I was wrong.

"There is something I have to tell you, and I need you to know how sorry I am to tell you this now, after all we have been through and all we have overcome," Carson said, holding both my hands in his.

"What is it? What's wrong?" I was scared to hear what he was about to say and fearful of where another confession might lead us.

"Abby, I'm sorry. Back when things were really bad, I was unfaithful to you," he confessed, still holding my hands.

"You had an affair?" I asked, letting go of him.

He reached for my hands again, but I kept them locked at my side.

"No. It wasn't like that. There wasn't one woman, there were many women. None of them I knew, all of them I paid."

"You slept with prostitutes?"

"Not exactly. I went to massage parlors where sexual favors could be bought. And when I wasn't going to parlors, I was using pornography instead."

I almost could not believe my ears. There were times when we would go months without intimacy, and I wondered if he was having an affair and sleeping with someone else, but I never even considered this.

"I'm so sorry for what I have done, but it was a long time ago, and I haven't done it since, and I would never do it again. I confessed to Michael and asked God for forgiveness. But, lately, God has been telling me to confess to you and ask for your forgiveness."

I did not know what to say to Carson, but I did what I felt compelled to do in that moment and reached for his hands again.

Had we gone too far to come back this time?

Had we made enough progress to see us through?

We stood together, not knowing what to do next.

ʘʘʘ

Carson

Abby definitely pulled away from me in the days after I confessed my sexual betrayal to her, and I tried to give her the space she needed. At times I feared we were back at the beginning and all our progress had been lost. I questioned God and his timing, but I still believed it was necessary and right to confess to Abby what I had done. I prayed for her forgiveness.

When Abby started to come around within a week of my confession, I saw God's timing had been perfect. A year before or even six months before, the outcome may not have been the same. But we both knew we had a lot to lose if we chose to walk away from what we'd managed to build together. Abby found it in her heart to forgive me, and I thanked God for freeing me from the secret when he did.

While coming to terms with what I did and how it affected our marriage, I began to think more about my father. I began to wonder about the new life he had chosen on the road home from Indiana and if there was any way my family and I could be part of that life.

With that in mind, I made plans to visit him for three days. By the second day of the visit, I chose to leave early. At 3 a.m., I was up writing him a letter that I wouldn't send until I returned home. I changed my flight and, long before the sun came up, drove to an airport where I could catch the first flight out.

I needed my father to know the pain I felt seeing him interact with his new family. I needed him to know the burden he had left me to carry in explaining to my own children and nieces and nephews where their grandfather had gone. The truth was painful and confusing enough for my brothers and me, let alone our young children.

THE ROAD TO RICHES

I'd hoped to mend our relationship and start anew, but seeing him with his new family made it harder to accept that he had chosen them over us. I ended my letter by telling him I hoped to rebuild our relationship one day. God has continued to give me the strength to forgive him and to hope that one day we'll be able to mend what has been broken.

❧❧❧

Abby

One day, Carson told me, "Someday I think God wants us to move to South Carolina."

I was blindsided. *Why South Carolina?* I thought. *We don't know anybody in South Carolina.*

But over the course of six months, we both decided we needed to take a vacation in South Carolina and check it out. We had both learned that seeking God and asking him to take control of our lives often ended up much better than any plans we made for ourselves.

During our trip, we felt sure that this was the place we needed to be.

We had no idea how we could move across the country. We still had our house, several of Carson's business ventures and other responsibilities. We'd made a friend on our trip, but we didn't know anyone else. Somehow, God provided every step of the way. We were able to rent out our house for a year and eventually sell it. In late 2012, we found ourselves on the road, on our way to moving to upstate South Carolina.

FOUND

That same year, we met Rob Rucci and his wife, Mary Beth, at a home school group for our children. We found out that they'd recently planted Upcountry Church, and we began visiting as a family.

At Upcountry Church, with a small congregation and a huge heart for the Lord, we began to deeply and truly worship God. Our obedience to God has given us constant joy.

It is unimaginable to me now that, as God's child, I once felt so little self-worth. I used to vomit in an attempt to rid myself of doubts, anxiety and insecurities. The only solace I thought I could find resulted in the abuse of my body and regurgitation of the very nutrients intended to feed and nourish me.

Today, I feel peace and know absolutely nothing is impossible through God. Despite years of attending church and learning Bible verses as a child and adolescent, it took me years to move from studying God to actually seeking him. God's power and love freed me from everything that once trapped me and changed everything about the way I approach the world today.

As a mother, a wife and a daughter, I became more whole with God's help. During the pregnancy with our third child, it was amazing to experience God's miracle growing inside me without fear. Bulimia no longer had a hold on me.

Carson and I decided, in moving to upstate South Carolina, to raise our children in a way that enables them to seek their own relationship with God, hoping they might learn from our mistakes. We embraced the move and our new church willingly, wholeheartedly and with joy, knowing without it, we would be lost.

৵৵৵

Carson

Soon after I met Rob, I found out he was doing some construction work on the cabin his family lived in, not far from our house, and needed some help with the renovations. Because of my experience in construction, I offered to help him out on his days off.

It wasn't long before we became a part of Upcountry Church — a small, loving congregation in Travelers Rest that welcomes people from all walks of life. We found a way to join in the celebration of God's love for us, his power to heal and his desire to set us free from the things that break us down and deaden our hope. We found a congregation that's so sincere about getting to know one another, there's a 15-minute break between the music and the preaching to talk with each other and build friendships and enjoy fellowship.

I had always idolized my house, my cars — my success. But God was teaching me not to love anything more than I loved him. Over the course of five years, we sold off the things that I used to be so proud of.

Abby and I are still imperfect people, but we've learned that obedience to God leads to freedom. Even if obeying God seems hard. It doesn't matter where God calls us to go — we're going.

FOUND

Our marriage was broken, but God used every step to heal the parts of us we didn't even know needed to be fixed.

I never imagined I would be living in South Carolina or that I'd be driving a 1970s pickup truck. I never would have expected to feel free of money or the need to earn more and more of it. Or to look at my children and know that I'm doing everything I can to encourage them to seek God in their lives. Most of all, I never would have expected to be in a marriage that exudes love, trust and forgiveness and has helped make me the man I am today.

Not everything happened as I once planned or turned out as I once hoped. But the path God put me on has been so much richer than the dream I once tried to buy for my family and myself.

HEALING IN FORGIVENESS

The Story of Dottie

Written by Arlene Showalter

"Hurry up, Dottie, or we'll be late." Mom popped her head in my bedroom, smiled and left.

I hurried to strap on my shiny black patent-leather Mary Jane shoes. We had few occasions to dress up where we lived. Today, my 16-year-old sister, Judy, would marry her 23-year-old beau, Carl. At 9 years old, this would be my first wedding.

We piled into Dad's car and bounced down the rutted, dusty road to Omak, Washington, a one-hour drive on a good day.

The road swung south and west. "Sure glad your sister didn't choose August to marry," Dad grumbled with a good-natured grin.

"How come?"

"We'd be tangled up in the crowds that come to see the Suicide Race."

"*Suicide Race?*"

This time Dad laughed out loud.

"Yes, the crazy tradition started before you were born, Dottie. The inspiration came from Indian tradition of braves showing off their skills, but now both cowboy and Indian riders race their horses down Suicide Hill. It has a

62-degree slope. After that, they race through the Okanogan River. People come from all over to watch the race."

The day of the wedding, the town seemed its tiny, almost-deserted self. We pulled up to the justice of the peace office, and Dad parked the car. We tumbled out and straightened our good clothes and made our way to the ceremony.

Dad owned thousands of acres of good timber which he harvested and prepared for market. His diesel-run mill stood near our two-story home. Rather than three beds and a bath, we lived in three beds and a *path*. Our one-hole comfort station (outhouse) stayed tucked from view down a trail and in the woods.

Kerosene provided our lighting, and we used wood for heating and cooking. My brothers fetched our daily water needs from our nearby stream. We rode the bus to school in town. We left before dawn and returned after dark. When snow piled as high as our windows, we didn't go at all.

Two occupations existed for the area boys: lumberjack or alfalfa farmer. Girls selected from one choice — marriage, and she'd better accomplish this before age 18 or risk being viewed as an *old maid*.

Mom married at 16, and Judy followed in her footsteps. Carl came from Canada, only a stone's throw to the north. He worked with Dad.

"You're getting quite a catch," Mom said. "He plays guitar and sings so nicely."

"And he's so handsome," Judy sighed.

"He's a hard worker," Dad said. "That's the most important thing."

After they said "I do," we bounced back home and began moving furniture around for new sleeping arrangements. My two brothers shared one bedroom, Judy and her new husband took the second and my younger sister Daisy and I shared a single bed in our parents' room.

I don't mind giving up my room. Now, I get to sleep with my best friend and sister, I thought as we moved our bed and belongings. *It'll be fun having Carl living with us all the time.*

ॐॐॐ

"I hate you!" Judy flung the words over her shoulder at Carl as she slammed out of the house and dashed into the woods. My feet cemented themselves to the kitchen floor. I dared a peek at Carl.

He remained at the table and took a slow sip of coffee. "She'll get over it." He smiled.

I relaxed.

After 15 minutes passed, Carl stood up and stretched. "You want to help me find your sister?"

"Of course." I tucked my small hand into his large, calloused one, and we trotted into the woods together. Carl veered right.

"I thought she went that way." I pointed left.

"Silly girl." Carl's laugh came easy. "You're only 9 years old. I saw her run this way."

FOUND

After walking another 20 minutes, I spotted some droppings and settled on my haunches to study them.

"I think it's deer," I said, standing up and turning toward Carl. He stood naked from the waist down and grinning.

"Don't be scared," he coaxed. "Come here."

I backed away, horrified at something I'd never seen before. My cheeks felt hot, and my breath came in bunches, as large, hot tears rolled down my cheeks.

"Come here," Carl demanded, steel edging his voice. He stepped forward. I stepped back. He grabbed my hand and pulled me close. Then he leaned in, almost touching my nose. "You tell anyone and you'll be in big trouble."

You don't have to worry about that. I wouldn't dream of telling anyone about what you just did.

ॐॐॐ

We would love to have Patty come spend the weekend here with Dottie.

I carefully delivered the note to my school friend, happy to be Mom's carrier pigeon. Nobody had telephones where we lived.

Patty happily took the note and bore it home. She returned the next day with her mother's response. *Yes, Patty can stay. I will send clothes with her on Friday. I hope the girls have a wonderful time.*

We rode the bus together on Friday, chattering like birds the full hour-plus ride to my house.

"We'll explore the woods tomorrow," I said. "I can show you my favorite spots."

We rushed through Mom's hearty breakfast the next morning. Patty and I wanted to enjoy every possible moment together until Monday morning rolled around.

We trotted into Dad's woods, inhaling the pungent odors of the white pine, Douglas fir and tamarack trees. We talked about life from our 11-year-old perspective.

"My dad says the Air Force is building a base close to us," I said.

"What's that?"

"I don't know. He said something about it being a radar station to make sure these 'commie guys' don't come and get us."

"Commie guys? What's that?"

"He said they're bad men who want to kill us," I said.

"Kill us? Why?"

I shrugged.

"That must be the place my sister Theresa and her friend Shirley were giggling about."

"Laughing that bad guys want to hurt us?" I stopped, horrified.

"No, they said something like it will bring young men to our area. More to choose from. Theresa's already 16. She's getting worried because she hasn't got a beau yet."

We laughed together and continued our meandering as we discussed bad people, eligible boys and marriage.

Suddenly I stopped. Frantically, I scoured the area. *Carl! This is where it all started.*

FOUND

"Come on, Dottie." Patty skipped on ahead. My feet refused to move, and I felt like fainting.

"What's wrong?" Patty ran back and grabbed my arm. "Dottie, tell me what's wrong!"

"Nothing." I fought for composure. "I guess I'm not used to running this far. I'm all right. I promise."

"Then let's head back." Patty looped her arm in mine. "We've been gone a long time, and I don't want your mom worrying about us and not letting me come back."

❧❧❧

I can't wait any longer. I have to go now. My heart pounded as I trotted to the family outhouse. *Maybe he didn't see me this time.* I quickened my pace, running the last few yards. I swung the door open, dashed inside and slapped it shut. I hooked it secure and then, only then, did I dare sit.

Before I could completely empty my bladder, I heard a noise. The hook lifted. I stared at its rise in frozen terror. *He's here.* I shrank against the hard wooden wall. *I wish I could die.*

Because Dad's sawmill was only about 100 yards from the house, Carl could easily keep me under constant surveillance.

Now, he stepped in and filled the small structure with his muscled body, as he had for the prior three years. No words passed between us as he satisfied his sadistic needs and slipped away, again leaving me smothered in silent shame.

In summertime, Daisy and I slept on a screened porch. I'd loved sleeping next to my beloved sister and listening to the night noises — until.

I'd lie with my eyes squeezed shut while *he* explored at will. Only concentrating on Daisy's easy breathing as she slept on — unaware of the nightmare occurring beside her — kept me focused on getting through one more time.

"We found a place to live," Judy announced. "I'm glad we'll finally be on our own after three years."

I willed my body to stay still, while my thoughts galloped. *Maybe I'll be safe now.*

"Daisy and I are driving into town this afternoon," Mom said, soon after Judy and Carl moved out. "Do you want or need anything?"

"Not this time. Have a safe trip."

"Thank you, dear." Mom gave my shoulder a gentle squeeze.

Before the sound of the car's engine died away, I heard the back door click. Carl advanced with the same threatening gleam in his eye. I stood like a statue, not needing the confines of a small outhouse to keep my body still.

Carl took — and left. Shame muzzled me in silence.

I would have prayed if I knew a real God existed. The few times I'd been exposed to pastors, they said strange things about strange beings I didn't know and then a person was married or was ready to bury.

School provided my only sanctuary from confusion,

dread and fear. I threw myself into my studies and excelled. Winter snows imprisoned me, and I longed for spring with more fervor every year.

"Your father and I are driving to Spokane today," Mom told me when I was 13. "We'll be gone two days. Judy and Carl will stay here and make sure you kids are okay."

My knees trembled. *He'll be back under our roof again. How can I bear it?*

The next morning I awakened burning up with fever. After Daisy left on the bus, Judy came back to where I lay in agony on the couch.

"I think we'd better take her to the hospital," she told Carl. "Come on, Dottie, put your clothes on." She handed me a skirt and blouse.

I screamed in pain. "I can't stand anything touching my skin."

"What are we going to do? You can't go in that ratty old bathrobe. I know. I have a lovely new robe. I'll have our brother drive me down to my place and get it." She touched my hand and smiled. "Carl will watch out for you until we get back."

Don't go … can't be alone … the pain, the pain … can't leave me … I hurt so bad … don't leave me. Please don't leave me.

The moment the sound of tires crunching faded, Carl came over to where I lay. Even my eyes hurt as I squeezed them shut. He towered over me for one eternal second before taking what he wanted. I was thankful that the blazing fever masked the pain.

❧ ❧ ❧

"She has rheumatic fever," I heard the doctor tell Judy. "We'll have to admit her."

I spent the next month battling the fever, wanting to get well while grateful for the Carl-free zone. *He can't touch me here.* I snuggled deep in the white sheets and blankets and drifted into a carefree deep and restful sleep. *I'm safe at last.*

Carl never touched me again.

❧ ❧ ❧

Okanogan Indians occupied our land first. Then traders built a post on the Kettle River, which grew into the town of Curlew after gold was discovered in the late 1800s. After depleting the mines, prospectors drifted on, and farmers and lumberjacks moved in.

The Air Force arrived in 1950. Fresh off World War II and the onset of the Korean Conflict, the secretary of defense authorized the Air Force to set up a "radar net" to monitor all air activity and warn fighter bombers in the event of an actual invasion.

Curlew Air Force Station, built on Bodie Mountain and minutes from the Canadian border, became one of 28 built-in strategic areas of the United States. Communism remained a remote concept in our area, while the influx of eligible bachelors electrified the local girls.

Because of its remote location, the Air Force provided its own superb food and entertainment and invited civilians to come and enjoy both. Their generosity offered us girls the opportunity to scope out soldiers from all over the United States.

Daisy began dating Charles, whom she met on the base.

"I'm going to run into the mess hall and get us some hamburgers," he said on one of our visits. "You girls sit tight."

Daisy and I chatted in his car — she in the front seat, and I in the back.

After a few minutes, Charles returned with a friend in tow.

"Daisy, Dottie, I want you to meet my good friend George from New Joisey."

"New *what*?"

"Jersey." George laughed. "He's poking fun at me because folks there say Joisey."

He hopped in the backseat next to me.

"So what do you think of Washington?" I asked.

"Sure is different from New Jersey. We have skyscrapers and huge cities and the ocean."

"We've never seen either," Daisy said. "Only pictures at school."

"I can't even imagine that. How do you manage up here in the boondocks?"

"I guess it's all we've ever known, so we don't know what we're missing," I said. "You have to admit the mountains are gorgeous. Sorta look like the pictures of the Alps we've seen at school, don't you think?"

"And our rolling hills. They smell so good when harvest time comes for alfalfa. Nothing like it."

"It's a whole different world," George agreed. "It just takes some getting used to."

"How long you plan on staying in the military?" I asked.

"Only until my stint is up in two years."

A few days later, Daisy informed me, "Charles tells me George is quite taken with you. I expect you'll be seeing him soon."

Shortly after that, George hiked down from the station to our house. Mom and Dad liked him from the start and approved of our dating.

"Look what I have!" George drove up, honking. "I finally bought a car. Let's celebrate. I'll drive you into town for supper and a movie."

"I'd *love* it."

"Would you marry me?" George asked a few months later as we sat in his car.

"Yes. I'd be happy to!"

Later that night, old memories threatened to slash my newfound joy into tattered ribbons. *I can't tell George. I have to tell George. I hate Carl! Why did he do that to me all those years? He had no right. I hate him.*

"I have to tell you something important," I said to

George as he prepared to go back to the base after his next visit.

"Of course." He wrapped an arm around me. I shrank back.

"What is it?" he whispered. "Come, let's go out on the porch, and you can tell me what's bothering you."

"I … I …" I stared at the countless stars winking and blinking above us.

"Tell me." George's tone stayed low and warm. "Whatever it is, I'm sure you'll feel better when you tell me."

"I'm not a virgin," I blurted. I dropped my head between my knees and sobbed.

"How? Why?" George pulled my head up and cradled it with his two hands. "Dottie, please tell me what happened."

"When Judy married Carl, they moved in with us. He started molesting me right away."

"I'm so sorry." George drew me into his arms. "Why didn't you tell your parents?"

"I couldn't. I was only 9 years old. I didn't understand what Carl was doing to me, but I knew it was wrong. Nobody *ever* talks about that kind of stuff around here. I couldn't do it — not because I was afraid of my parents, they're wonderful people — but the shame just about swallowed me whole."

George held my sobbing body until I sagged against him. "Tell me," he whispered.

"I lived in constant tension. Every minute of every day

I wondered when he would attack me next. This went on every week from 9 years old until …"

"It's okay. You're safe with me."

"I got really sick two years ago, when I was 13. My sister went to her house for a few minutes to get her nice bathrobe for me to wear to the hospital." I took a few deep breaths. "As soon as she left, Carl raped me one last time."

George allowed me to sob for a few more minutes before saying, "And your parents have *no* idea? None?"

"None."

"Excuse me." George stood up and opened the front screen. "They're going to find out — right now."

I huddled in a miserable heap until he returned.

"I don't believe it," he said, as he sat next to me again. "I just can't believe it."

"What did they say?" I asked.

"Well, first, they looked utterly and completely shocked, but they believed your story. They said you're not the sort of person to make up such a fantastic tale."

"I'm glad of that. And glad they finally know."

"But, here's the kicker. Your mom said you know how explosive your sister is and if she found out what Carl did, she'd go off. She has four kids. She can't afford to leave him. Your mom said you have to keep quiet about it!"

Pain — worse than what Carl had done — ripped through me. "How can they love Judy more than me?" I wailed. "How could they ask me to keep my mouth shut just so she can keep on living her life?"

"I'm with you, Dottie. You've lived with it this long.

FOUND

And since Carl has left you alone since, I'll help you get through the next year. After we get married, you'll come live on base with me."

I threw my arms around his neck. "I love you! With you on my side, I can do it."

We married the summer before my senior year.

"You'll finish high school, even though we're married," George said. "The bus will come to the base and pick you up."

"I'd like that."

"And, right after you graduate, my enlistment is up, and we can go home to New Jersey. You never have to see Carl again."

I'm not sure even New Jersey is far enough away from that monster. I hate him so much.

"It'll be fun to see more of America," I said, shaking off the sudden anger that flared in my heart. "But I think I'll miss these mountains."

"You will see the ocean, too. That can make up for the mountains, I think."

ৡৡৡ

This is it. I am leaving forever. My family. My mountains. My home. My heart thudded as each jet engine started and warmed.

The aircraft thundered down the runway. I clutched my 5-month-old son to my chest and breathed deeply. Our bodies thrust back against our seats as the plane sliced through the clouds. I jumped when I heard what sounded like rocks rolling against its belly, yet we raced on — and up.

With a final rend, the jet freed itself of all clouds. I plastered my nose against the window and gazed at the land far, far below us. Farms, rivers, plains and cities crept passed as we roared toward George's home.

My beloved mountains look like anthills below us. The Great Plains look like a patchwork quilt, and those cities look like tiny clusters of wooden blocks.

The buildings grew larger and larger as we descended toward the airport in New Jersey. First, they grew knee-sized, then taller than I and, finally, as earth rushed to meet us, towered above us.

"They look as tall as our mountains!" I tried to take it all in — the cars choking the paved roads, the buildings blocking the sun. "And people *everywhere.*"

How can I ever adjust to this? A trip to the moon couldn't be any stranger than this.

"This is where you grew up?" I asked George, soon after we settled in with his parents. "How did you ever sleep with all this noise?"

"You get used to it."

"Maybe, but it's going to take me some time."

"When I first arrived at the air station, I couldn't sleep for the silence," he said, laughing.

George got a college degree and landed a good job with IBM. Over the years, IBM transferred him to the

Philadelphia area and then to a town 30 minutes south of Pittsburgh.

"I know you grew up in the city," I told George, "but now that I've lived in several cities, I think it's healthier for our children to grow up like I did in the country."

"I agree," he said. "There are lots of rural areas around here. We can start looking for property."

We shopped around and found an old dilapidated farmhouse on 50 acres. "This would be perfect for the boys."

"Let's put an offer in," George said.

৵৵৵

I heard a knock on the door several days after we'd settled in.

"Hi, I'm Pastor Black."

Pastor? Here? Did somebody die?

"Hello. Can I help you?"

"I'm just here to welcome you to the neighborhood."

Oh. "Thank you."

"Do you mind if I ask you a question?"

"No. Go ahead."

"Are you saved?"

Saved from what? A flood? A fire? "I don't know what you mean."

"Saved. You know, by the blood of Jesus."

Blood of Jesus? I stepped back, horrified.

"I don't know about any man named Jesus being killed."

"I'm sorry. I didn't mean to frighten you. Come to church next Sunday, and you can learn all about Jesus."

"Why? Is someone in the neighborhood getting married? Or did somebody die?"

"*What?*" Now, he looked confused.

"Isn't that what church is for? Marrying and burying?"

"No." He laughed. "It's for more than that."

I mulled over his words after he left. *Who is this Jesus, and what did he mean by being saved?* The only Jesus I knew about was in cussing. *Now this preacher is trying to tell me that Jesus is a real person and not only that, he came to "save" me? Save me from what?*

A few days later, I answered another knock.

"Good morning. I'm Pastor Johns from the church just up the way." He waved in the opposite direction of the other pastor. "And this is my lovely wife, Mrs. Johns. We've come to welcome you to the neighborhood."

They're a bit friendlier than over-busy city folks. I do appreciate that. "Please, won't you come in?" I bounced Timmy in my arms. "May I offer you some coffee?"

"That sounds lovely," Mrs. Johns said. "We sure are pleased you bought this old house. I've always admired it. With just a little TLC, you'll have it looking like a showplace, I'm sure."

"Thank you. That's why we bought it. That and we wanted to raise our kids in the country."

"How many children do you have?"

"This one is the youngest of five. The eldest graduates high school this year."

"You are blessed," Mrs. Johns said.

Blessed? These people talk funny, but they seem nice.

We traded stories for a little while. I told them about growing up in the sticks of Eastern Washington, how I met New Jersey-raised George.

"I like it here in Pennsylvania better than New Jersey, though. I do miss the ocean. I saw it for the first time when I was 17, after George got out of the Air Force and we moved in with his folks in New Jersey. I felt so tiny against its vastness."

I also remember thinking even that wouldn't be enough water to wash away all the shame Carl heaped on me. I hate him so much!

We chatted a little longer.

"Do you mind if I ask you a question?"

Sounds like the other preacher man. Do they all have a script?

"Not at all." I popped my son in his booster seat and scattered some crackers on the table.

"Are you saved?"

Saved? Here we go again. What is it with these people? Is there something about Pennsylvanians I need to know?

"Saved from what?" I asked.

"Saved from sin. Saved from being lost. Jesus said, 'I came to seek and save that which was lost.'"

Jesus again. Just like the other preacher. Who is this Jesus fellow, anyway?

"Do you know Jesus?"

"No, can't say that I do. Does he live around here?

There was another preacher here a few days ago, and he asked me the same thing."

"No, no. Jesus is God's son. He came to earth to die for all of us."

"Why?"

"Because we're all sinners. And sin separates us from God."

God? You mean, he's a real person, too?

My face burned. "I don't know anything about God or Jesus."

"Please, don't be embarrassed." Mrs. Johns touched my hand. "We will be happy to tell you all about Jesus if we're not taking you from your work."

Mr. Johns began explaining how this man named Jesus was born from a virgin — *is that even possible?* — by the Holy Spirit — *whatever, whoever that is* — and his whole purpose was to save us from this thing called sin.

"Do you understand what sin is?"

"Not really."

"Sin is doing bad things, thinking wrong thoughts — things that separate us from a holy God. Do you think you are a sinner?"

Bad things? I know all about bad things. Like what Carl did to me. Those were horrible things. I hate him so much. I wonder if hating him comes under the "bad thoughts"?

"I'm not sure what you mean."

"We all do bad things, Dottie. Some can be really big, like murder or drunkenness."

FOUND

Or molestation. "I've never done anything like that."

"Of course not. We know that. But, sin can also be as small as telling tiny white lies, or gossiping or anger or hatred."

Hatred? I struggled to breathe.

"Dottie, how would you like to go to a prayer meeting with Mrs. Johns and me?"

"A prayer meeting? What is a prayer meeting?"

"It's simply where a few people get together and talk to God."

"Why?"

"To ask him to clean up our hearts. To ask for help in our daily lives. To tell him how much we love and appreciate him."

"Well, I suppose I could do that."

"Wonderful. We'll swing by and pick you up on Wednesday, around 6:30."

"Okay. I'll be ready."

Pastor and Mrs. Johns escorted me into a home where fewer than a dozen women sat in the living room. He held up one hand. "Before we get started," he said, "I'd like to go around the room and have each of you give a brief testimony of what Jesus means to you."

"Jesus saved me from alcoholism."

"Jesus healed our marriage."

"Jesus comforted me when my mother died last year."

I wanted to evaporate. *These people are talking about this Jesus like they know him personally. And Pastor*

Johns said he was God who came to earth and was born from a virgin — I still can't believe that's possible — and then died a horrible death, and it was all for me.

"Dottie, do you own a Bible?" Mr. Johns asked as they drove me home.

"No. What is a Bible?"

"The Bible is God's word to us. It will tell you all about Jesus."

"That would be wonderful." *It seems I couldn't go anywhere without hearing about this Jesus, so I may as well read about him.*

"We'll bring you one next week. Is it okay if we come and visit again?"

"Sure. I look forward to it."

"We're holding the prayer meeting at our church next Wednesday. Would you like to come?"

"Okay."

After the meeting, a few ladies gathered around me. More talked about what this Jesus meant to them.

"I want to know Jesus the way these ladies do. He seems so real to you all."

"That's because he is real."

"And he promised never to leave us."

"I want to know him!"

"Jesus came because we are all imperfect, and we all fall short of God's glory. Only Jesus can save us from sin and from ourselves because he was born and lived 100 percent sinless. When we believe in him, we are saved

from sin, and we become sons and daughters of God,"
Pastor Johns explained. "Do you want to accept Jesus into
your heart and life right now?"

"Yes. Yes!"

As we prayed, I clutched my new Bible to my chest
and sobbed. God's peace flooded over me, more real than
anything I'd ever felt in my life. I felt clean. I felt at peace. I
felt *safe*.

ॐॐॐ

"Timmy, listen to this. 'As Jesus went from there, two
blind men followed him …'" I began reading in Matthew,
chapter 9.

"What's blind?" he asked.

"It means they couldn't see. Like this." I put my hands
over his eyes. Timmy shook his head.

"I don't like that."

"No, I'm sure you don't. These poor men couldn't
even work because they couldn't see anything. Now, let
me read more. Let's see, where was I? Oh, yes, here. They
were saying to Jesus, 'Have mercy on us.'"

"Then what?" Timmy asked.

"Jesus asked, 'Do you believe that I am able to do
this?'"

"What did they say?" Timmy left his toys to lean on
my knee.

"They said yes, so Jesus touched their eyes and —
guess what?"

"They could see!" Timmy bounced on the balls of his feet. "Right, Mommy?"

"Yes, Jesus made their eyes well so they could see."

"Yay, Jesus! I love Jesus!" Timmy shouted, dashing around the room.

"Guess what, Daddy?" Timmy said as we gathered for dinner.

"What's that, Tiger?"

"Jesus made blind men see!"

George looked at me and rolled his eyes.

"Do you have to indoctrinate our kids with that drivel?" he asked when we were alone in our bedroom. "We lived fine before this Jesus stuff. Why do you need it now?"

But I couldn't satisfy my appetite to learn more and more about my new friend Jesus.

I read the Bible every possible moment, careful to tuck it away before George returned from work. I went to church at every opportunity and took every Bible class I could.

And, to George's discomfort, in time all five of our children embraced the same Jesus.

"Our Father in heaven, hallowed be your name ..." I read what is known as *The Lord's Prayer* for the first time in my life. "Your kingdom come, your will be done on earth as it is in heaven." *Wouldn't that be wonderful if we all lived like Jesus?*

"Give us today our daily bread." *Thank you for George's good job. It definitely meets our financial needs.*

FOUND

"Forgive us our debts, as we also have forgiven our debtors." *Makes sense.*

"And lead us not into temptation, but deliver us from the evil one." *Amen to that!*

"For if you forgive men when they sin against you, your heavenly father will also forgive you. But if you do not forgive men their sins, your father will not forgive your sins."

"Oh, dear," I cried out loud as tears rolled down my cheeks. I studied the rolling hills outside our picture window. "How can I ever forgive what Carl did to me? It's just too much to ask."

I prayed. I wept. I prayed more. *I'm so sorry, God, but I just don't have the strength to forgive him.*

How can you not forgive him? I sensed God's voice deep in my heart.

"He made me so scared all the time. He had no right!"

You're correct, Dottie. He had no right. But Jesus died for everybody or he died for nobody.

"But it's so hard," I sobbed.

So was watching my son die.

"God, I want your forgiveness for all my sins, so I have to forgive Carl. I can't do it on my own, but I do give you permission to change my heart, because I don't have the ability to do it on my own."

స~~~

HEALING IN FORGIVENESS

I made plans to fly home to Washington shortly after my discussion with God about the forgiveness issue.

My stomach flip-flopped as the plane soared over the Great Plains and then over my beloved mountains before touching down in Spokane. *God help me!* I prayed as I made my way to the exit.

I stared up the escalator. Mom, Judy *and* Carl descended toward me. My breath caught. *I need you right now, God. More than I've ever needed you before.*

"Hi, Mom." We hugged.

"Good to see you, Judy." Another hug.

I looked up at Carl and opened my arms for a hug. At that very moment, power surged through me. I wrapped my arms around his neck and pulled him close enough to whisper in his ear.

"I forgive you."

Carl stepped back. Bewilderment spread across his face. Joy flooded my heart. *He did it. He really did it. God changed my heart so I could forgive.* The chains of terror and shame and hatred dissolved into a sea of forgiveness, never to torment me again.

❧❧❧

Thank you, Jesus, that we are all together for such a special day. My heart filled with gratitude as my husband and all five of our children sat with me in church on Easter Sunday. *This is a special day, first, because we are celebrating your resurrection and second, that I have all my family here. How much has changed since I first committed my life to you 11 years ago. My boys have all done the same and serve you with faithfulness. I know it's only a matter of time until George commits to following you as well. For now, I'm just thankful he's here in church with us.*

The pastor ended his message and invited anyone who wanted to give his or her heart to Jesus to please step forward and come to the front of the church.

My hand flew to my mouth as my husband stood up and began walking toward the pastor. George? *George?* My heart pounded.

One by one, all of our kids rose and followed their father down the aisle. They formed a semi-circle around him while the pastor prayed.

Tears ran down my face as I gazed on that precious sight, and I began quoting to myself: "When the Lord brought back the captives to Zion, we were like men who dreamed. Our mouths were filled with laughter, our tongues with songs of joy. Then it was said among the nations, 'The Lord has done great things for them.' The Lord has done great things for us, and we are filled with joy. Restore our fortunes, O Lord, like streams in the Negev. Those who sow in tears will reap with songs of joy. He who goes out weeping, carrying seed to sow, will return with songs of joy, carrying sheaves with him" (Psalm 126).

You did it, Heavenly Father, just as you promised me you would. You have brought George in, and now our family is truly complete.

HEALING IN FORGIVENESS

❧❧❧

"Can you come take care of Judy?" Carl called me. By this time, IBM had transferred George to South Carolina. Judy had developed cancer, and I flew home every year to see her. "She's not expected to live out the week. Can you stay until the end?"

Why didn't he ask Daisy? I wondered as the jet rushed me back to Washington. *She still lives in the area.*

I settled in, and Daisy came over every day to help.

"Wake up." Daisy bent over me, shaking me. "Judy is screaming for you. She even yelled your name."

I raced up the steps and sat close by my sister. "Judy." I bent close and whispered in her ear. "Can you hear me?"

"Uhnnnn."

"This is Dottie. Do you know me?"

"Uhnnn-hunnn."

"Judy, do you want to go be with Jesus when you die?"

"Uhnnnn."

Quickly I sketched out God's love and redemption through Jesus — his life, death and resurrection.

"Do you understand, Judy?"

"Uhnnnn."

"Do you want to accept Jesus in your heart?"

"Uhnnnn-hunnn."

I prayed in her ear until I felt my sister's body relax.

Thank you, Heavenly Father, for the privilege of bringing my sister into your family. I know that she is safe in your care now. And now I understand why you prompted Carl to ask me to take care of her. I'm the only Christian she knows.

I knew in my heart that the next time she opened her eyes, she would be seeing Jesus.

SOMETHING GOOD
The Story of Justin
Written by Joy Steiner Moore

The moonlight cast long shadows on the ceiling of my parents' bedroom, and I just lay there, completely still, listening to the summer crickets sing their steady song outside the window. I'd tried to fall asleep in my own bed, but my mind kept mulling over the events of the day — how frail my dad looked, his eyes staring blankly at the hospital wall as he struggled to breathe. Whether I was seeking comfort or familiarity I wasn't sure, but in the middle of the night I had wandered to Mom and Dad's empty bed hoping to quiet my mind and drift off to sleep.

But sleep wouldn't come. My thoughts kept roaming to my father, the strongest man I knew — the hardest-working man I knew. The commercial fisherman and farmer.

He's going to beat this, I told myself. *He has to.*

My mom hadn't been home in days. She'd been stalwart through Dad's illness, a constant presence at his bedside, spending night after night at the hospital. I always knew she was strong, but Dad's cancer diagnosis proved it. She was his constant advocate and caregiver, ever vigilant and waiting for the day that he'd be better and could come back home at last.

Car headlights interrupted my thoughts, dancing on the ceiling as a vehicle pulled up the driveway.

FOUND

Mom's home.

I wondered what it meant. I panicked.

Maybe she's just taking a break, I tried to convince myself. *She probably needs some sleep.*

I heard the front door open, so I got up and went out to the living room. There my mom stood, embracing my older brother Paul, tears streaming down her face. I rarely saw my mom cry, if ever. I felt frozen in place, trying to force my brain to comprehend.

Mom saw me then, and a fresh wave of tears hit her.

"Your father died, Justin," she said through her sobs.

The words were so — final. I felt my mind trying to accept their awful meaning. I made my way back to my parents' room and lay back down in the darkness.

This can't be happening. Dads aren't supposed to die when you're 16. He was supposed to get better.

But he didn't. My father was dead.

❧❧❧

The way my older brother tells it, I almost died of a fever when I was just a toddler. We had a little 10-acre farm in Lancaster, Pennsylvania — Amish country. My dad raised pigs and grew corn, and Mom had a produce stand out by the road. My parents and brother were out working in the fields one day, while we smaller kids stayed with my grandmother in her nearby trailer. When my mom got word that I suddenly stopped breathing and even turned blue, my brother says she took off running across the field, faster than he had ever seen. My fever was so high that the doctors didn't even tell her the temperature, to keep from alarming her. I eventually recovered, but the freakish fever cost me about half of my hearing in my right ear.

For the most part, life on the farm was fun. I remember bouncing atop hay bales, playing on the farm equipment and spending summers running through the pig sty with snow boots to keep my feet from getting muddy.

But I was such a shy kid that I nearly failed kindergarten. The teacher was mean, and she terrified me. So when I dropped my blue crayon and it rolled beneath the teacher's desk, I was too afraid to ask her permission to get it.

I'm just fine sitting here and not getting yelled at, I thought to myself, having seen another student get reprimanded harshly.

When I got home, I went through my brothers' and sister's crayons in search of a blue one, without success. So from then on, whenever I needed to color something blue, I would combine other colors to try to get as close to blue as possible. As a result, my teacher thought I wasn't learning the differences between colors and gave me low marks on my report card. When my mom finally figured out what was going on, she marched me into the classroom and, in an effort to help me overcome my shyness, made me ask the teacher for my blue crayon hidden just under her desk. My parents didn't coddle me.

FOUND

They wanted me to be my best self and were consistent in trying to help me get past my shyness and gain confidence.

When I was 5, we left the green rolling hills of Pennsylvania and settled in Palm Bay, Florida, so my dad could pursue commercial fishing. Florida definitely had its perks. My family made a real effort to do all the touristy things, like Disney World, SeaWorld and the Kennedy Space Center.

My mom and dad were dedicated churchgoers and taught me all about the Bible from the time I was a baby. I understood that I wasn't perfect, that I was prone to doing things that made God unhappy, and I knew that I didn't want to go to hell when I died. But when I was 6 years old, I suddenly felt compelled to do something about it — to give my life to Jesus. We were sitting in church, and when they invited people to come to the altar, I bravely walked to the front of the room. I didn't know what to say or do, but I knew that I wanted to be God's child — that if I accepted that Jesus had taken my punishment already, I could be part of God's pure and spotless family. My Sunday school teacher met me there and went through the Bible with me to make sure I understood what I was doing. I knew all the stories already. I was pretty certain I was doing the right thing. And from that point forward, I felt different. I felt happy knowing that the bad things I had done were already taken care of and that I had a secure place in God's family. From then on, I had a distinct feeling that God was on my side.

Later that year, my first grade class stood outside our

school and faced north, where the *Challenger* space shuttle was launching about 30 miles away. We'd toured the space shuttle on a field trip earlier in the school year, so we'd looked forward to the event. My music teacher turned his radio on so he could hear the news coverage, and we watched as the shuttle lifted into the sky and then split from its rocket in a fiery explosion, leaving a jagged trail of billowing white smoke. At the age of 6, I didn't know what a shuttle liftoff was supposed to look like.

"It blew up! It blew up!" my music teacher yelled, shocked.

We gazed into the sky, stunned at the sudden turn of events. It was a surreal experience that made a lasting impression on me.

꙯꙯꙯

We moved to the North Carolina coast that summer, and my parents bought a little blue cinderblock house not far from the beach. My grandma lived in a little trailer next to us, and we kids would often drop in to play board games with her. In the summers, my dad would take me out on his fishing boat to go clamming and show me the value of hard work. I knew the guy at the fish house would pay me about 10 cents per clam, so when I felt like I'd made the amount of money I hoped to make, I'd get to play in the boat for the rest of the day.

In the spring of 1995, when I was a sophomore in high school, Dad pulled a muscle in his back. He'd had trouble with his back before, but this time it seemed to be taking longer to heal. After a few weeks of soreness, he finally went to the doctor and came home with that scary diagnosis — cancer.

From the beginning, I felt optimistic. Dads aren't supposed to die, and my dad would be no exception. I remained confident that he would get better. He was a good man — I couldn't picture a life where he wasn't present. Even after he was admitted to the hospital, I knew God would heal him. After all, our entire church was praying.

An older lady from the church came to visit him in his hospital room.

"We're praying for you," she said, patting Dad's hand. "We're believing you're going to get better."

"You wanna see Jesus before me or something?" my dad responded. He was not afraid of death. He knew where he was going when he died.

On June 21, just two days after my mom's birthday, he passed away. The shock was a lot for me to absorb. I actually felt numb.

How is this going to work, God?

I remembered that the Bible said that "in all things God works for the good of those who love him, who have been called according to his purpose," and I believed that was true. I had no reason to doubt him. I knew in my heart that God would come through for my family. But as I stretched out my tall teenage frame on my parents' bed, listening to my mom's and siblings' quiet sobs in the other room, I wondered how in the world we would survive on my mom's income. I honestly felt like God had his work cut out for him. And I saw my life laid out before me — bleak, sad and absent of my wonderful father.

〜〜〜

The saddest thing for me was knowing that my mom had to live without him. They'd been together since she was 14, and they'd been best friends, as well as spouses. My heart ached for her.

"Are you going to remarry?" Mom's friends would ask.

"My husband was all I've known," she'd respond with a sad shrug. "I don't care to be with anyone else."

We got through the funeral and, despite the gigantic hole in our hearts, settled into our "new normal," in a sense — survival mode.

My oldest brother, Paul, was 28 and already lived five miles away on his own. Mom returned to her full-time job as a cook at the hospital, and in August, my other brother Will started as a freshman at Liberty University in Lynchburg, Virginia, while my older sister Julie and I prepared for our high school band competition in Charlotte. It was important to my mom that we each continue in our various activities and keep ourselves busy. We'd always been her priority.

A couple days before the band competition, Will expressed interest in coming down from college to watch it. My mom decided she'd drive up to Lynchburg and get him, then they'd drive down to Charlotte together in time for the competition. In the meantime, Julie and I had to stay and perform in our school's halftime show at the Friday night football game before traveling to Charlotte with the band.

Right before the game started, I noticed Julie standing with Paul and his girlfriend over by themselves. Julie bawled. Paul tried to comfort her. I set my trombone in its case and jogged over to see what was going on.

"Mom and Will have been in an accident," Paul said. "We need to go to Virginia. Pack up your stuff. We've gotta go."

We stopped by the house long enough to throw some clothes into suitcases and then headed out. We drove six hours to Danville, Virginia, and arrived at the hospital about 2 a.m. on Saturday morning.

Will met us at the entrance and walked us back to the ICU. Miraculously, he'd escaped serious injury, but Mom suffered from internal bleeding.

"Her vitals are stable, though," Will whispered as we rushed through the halls.

"What happened?" Julie asked.

"I was driving, and we were sitting at a stoplight waiting to turn. The other guy lost control and hit us head-on."

We arrived at Mom's room and entered quietly. I sucked in my breath at the sight of her banged-up body. She was unconscious, and all of us kids gathered around her bed. I reached out and gently squeezed her motionless hand.

"I love you, Mom," I choked out.

We stayed like that, surrounding our sleeping mother, feeling helpless. Mom was our rock, even more so in the three months since Dad died. She was an amazing woman. It wasn't easy to see her injured and unresponsive.

But, to our shock, at 2:20 a.m., the heart monitor gradually slowed down and flat-lined, and Mom was gone.

෴෴෴

This can't be happening! This can't be happening!

I pushed through the ICU doors and walked up and down the halls of the hospital, just to get away. I dealt with things in my own way, and being alone was key. I felt stunned at the direction my life had suddenly taken — at the finality of death — and I needed some time to process everything. In the middle of the night, most patients slept, the halls dark and quiet. I found solace in a small waiting room, where I sank into a chair. Grief overwhelmed me.

After a while, the hospital chaplain came looking for me. He tried to offer comfort, but I wasn't in the mood.

"Look, you don't have to comfort me," I told him. "I don't have any problems with God. I know he's going to take care of me. It's just — they're gone, you know? What do you want me to say?"

I leaned forward in my chair and threaded my fingers together, sighing heavily. In addition to the unimaginable sadness I experienced, I was exhausted, and the last thing I wanted was to make conversation with a stranger. The chaplain placed an awkward hand on my shoulder.

"Okay, son. I understand. I'll be praying for you."

I don't know how long I stayed there. There was a lot to think about. In the course of three months, I lost both of my parents. I was only 16 years old. I felt detached and removed from everything. The thread that tied me to the world had been snapped.

Who the heck do I go to for advice — for anything? How am I going to keep a roof over my head?

When I finally wandered back to my siblings, Will was describing his final hours with Mom — how her last words to him were, "Everything's going to be okay," as they loaded her onto a stretcher and into the ambulance.

A small amount of joy passed through me at the thought that Mom was reunited with Dad in heaven. As much as I missed Dad, I could only imagine the depths of Mom's grief in those weeks without him. It must have seemed like hell for her. And now, graciously, her hell was over. Though I'm sure she wouldn't have *chosen* to leave her kids to fend for themselves, for her, I believed everything was, in fact, okay. Actually, it was good.

༈༈༈

The big question remaining was, of course, what would happen to the two of us still living at home. Julie only had one year of high school left, and I had two.

Our aunt and uncle from Pennsylvania drove down to our house to help us deal with everything.

"Let Julie and Justin move in with us," my aunt offered. "We have plenty of room."

But Paul remembered what it was like to have to move and leave all his friends in the middle of high school, and he didn't want to put us through that after just losing both our parents. Also, though he'd been living a party lifestyle in recent years, Dad and Mom's deaths had sobered him up a bit, and he had matured, realizing how short life is.

"You know, Justin's only got two years left of high school," Paul answered, mulling it over. "I think I'll just move back in. It'd be best if we all stayed together."

And that's exactly what he did. Paul moved in, and we all set up house, like in the TV show *Party of Five*. In the three months she outlived Dad, Mom took out a life insurance policy on herself, which helped tremendously with paying for the house. People brought meals by, and we just tried to keep on living. We continued to go to church every Sunday. I kept up in band and baseball, though I sat the bench because I didn't have my parents advocating with the coach for my playing time, like other kids did.

"Do you ever get mad at God?" friends at church asked often.

"No, why?" I had overcome my shyness to become a very straight-forward person.

"Well, you lost both your parents."

"Look, we're talking about the God so powerful that he spoke the universe into existence. He created me. He gave me incredible parents. Why would I get mad at him? It's not going to do any good. He's on my side, and he always has been."

FOUND

ન્જ્જ્જ્જ

When I graduated from high school in 1997, Paul insisted I go to college in order to make something of my life. I went for one semester at the local community college and somehow ended up on my Western Civilization professor's bad side. I found school utterly annoying, and I just wasn't motivated to make it work.

Life's too short, I thought. *Dad worked so hard. It's work, work, work, and then what? There are other things I want to do with my life. I don't need to waste my time in a classroom.*

So I quit school and started detailing boats for a living. In the evenings and on weekends, I played ball with some guys at a nearby basketball court, which happened to be on the property of a church. As people started arriving for the evening church service one Sunday, we ended our game, and some of the other guys started heading inside the building. I got ready to go home.

"Come on in and join us!" a middle-aged woman said, walking toward me, a huge smile across her face. We talked for a few minutes, and she was so personable and friendly that I couldn't resist her invitation.

After that, I decided to keep attending that church. There were a lot of guys and girls my age, and I enjoyed the youth meetings. We spent our free time shooting hoops with the youth pastor, and since I knew a few of the guys already, I developed a great group of friends in a short amount of time.

SOMETHING GOOD

The lady who invited me in that first day was Cathy. She had a daughter in the youth group and took an interest in all of us, letting us hang out at her house quite a bit. Cathy spent a lot of time talking with each of us, sharing her wisdom. She became a good friend to me in a motherly sort of way.

I also started dating a girl in the youth group named Kendra. We dated on and off for two years before I found out through some mutual friends that she was secretly dating one of my best friends on the side.

When I approached her about it, she denied it, which made me even angrier. Why couldn't she just tell me the truth? As far as I was concerned, Dan could have her. I moved on.

Work hit a slow time for me, so I made the mistake of taking a job working for Kendra's dad, Mr. Lawson. He didn't completely trust Kendra or Dan, so being the protective father that he was, he spent his days trying to fish for information about their relationship from me.

I didn't want to be rude, but as politely as possible, I told him that I didn't know anything about them. She wasn't my problem anymore. She was his. I just needed to do my job. Mr. Lawson seemed to respect that, though he was disappointed.

One afternoon, I stopped by Cathy's house to see if anyone from the youth group was hanging out. But she stopped me from going past the front room.

"Yes, everyone's over here," Cathy said quietly. "But apparently, Mr. Lawson is making Kendra break up with

Dan, and the kids all seem to think it's your fault. They think you badmouthed them to her dad."

"What? That's crazy. I haven't said a thing to him."

"I know, Justin," she said kindly. "But everyone's pretty riled up about it. They're saying they want to fight you."

I chuckled. I was so much bigger than any of them.

"You know what?" Cathy crossed the room to the telephone. "We'll call Kendra's dad right now and see if we can get this straightened out."

"Oh, no, that's okay," I argued. "I've moved on. It doesn't matter."

But Cathy insisted I stay until we get everything sorted out. She convinced Mr. Lawson to come over and help clear the air. In her opinion, every moment was a teaching opportunity. She believed in facing problems head-on and not allowing gossip to infiltrate the group.

As Mr. Lawson took a seat on the sofa, the other kids entered the room. Kendra wasn't even there, but I could feel the tension mounting. They all eyed me suspiciously, even some of my closest friends.

How can they believe Kendra's lies? Don't they trust me? This is so messed up.

"Listen," Mr. Lawson began. "I don't know what's going on here. But I will be the first to tell you, Justin's the best friend y'all have. I've tried to get every bit of info out of him since he's worked for me, and he won't say a word."

The truth was out, and Mr. Lawson reassured

everyone that he was only making Dan and Kendra break up because he didn't feel right about the relationship. I don't know whether or not my friends had a change of heart about me, but I suddenly saw all of them in a different light.

These people have supposedly been my friends for two years, yet they believed what someone else said about me over what they knew about my character. I don't have room in my life for stuff like this.

I headed home, thoroughly depressed that my friends let me down. My friendships were important to me. With my parents gone, and since I had quit college, hanging out with the youth group had been a nice distraction for me. It kept me busy, and it gave me something to look forward to when I got off work each day.

But they're not really my friends. I can't trust them.

I suddenly felt incredibly lonely. But I knew I'd rather stay at home and watch a movie with my sister than hang out with people I couldn't trust.

Over the next few weeks and months, I did stay home more. The entire situation reminded me of a particular story in the Bible about Jesus' disciple Peter. Jesus told Peter to get out of the boat and come to him, and when he did, he walked on the water toward Jesus. As long as his eyes were on Jesus, he was fine. But the moment he looked away and started getting distracted by the wind and waves, he began to sink. I felt like that was my problem, too — I got distracted by so many things in my life that I didn't keep my eyes on Jesus. I'd been so distracted by friends, basketball, you name it — that I, too, had begun to sink. I had been doing my own thing, killing time, living somewhat aimlessly, with no focus on God.

I remembered one of my favorite scriptures: "Seek the kingdom of God above all else, and live righteously, and he will give you everything you need." I was 20 years old, and I suddenly felt my mindset pivot. I didn't want my life to be aimless and pointless. I put my eyes on Jesus. I decided to put God first.

ॐॐॐ

I continued to be involved in the church, but my focus became much different. I wanted to please God — I wasn't there to just "hang" anymore.

One night, Cathy was scheduled to speak in front of the youth group, and she asked if she could use a story about me as an example. I had no idea what it was about, but I agreed.

"In 1995, I read a newspaper article," Cathy began. "The article was about a family who lost their father to cancer and their mother in a car accident, just three months apart. My heart broke for the four kids they left behind, so I called the pastor of the church they attended, and I asked him if there was anything I could do for the family. The pastor assured me that they were a strong family — that they had a good support group and they were going to be fine. But he said, 'Just pray for them.' So I did. Two years later, Justin just happened to be playing basketball on the church property, and when I invited him into the service, he walked right through the doors of this church and became an integral part of this church family. I didn't know yet that he was one of the kids I'd been praying for. But when I did figure it out, it was amazing to me that God had brought him to this particular church, and that after praying for him all that time, God allowed me to meet him and to actually get to be part of his life."

The story was incredible. I hadn't known that about Cathy. I felt overwhelmed by God's goodness to care for me through the prayers of a stranger and then later to bring her into my life as a mentor and support. Even in the weeks before her talk, she and I discussed the possibility of me going back to college. She was a true friend who cared about my relationship with God and believed that God had a plan for my life.

Cathy went on to tell us that she'd just been diagnosed with cancer, but that as she had seen in my situation, she knew that God always worked everything out for good. She faced her fight bravely, her future safely in God's hands.

It was an emotional evening for me. I knew that cancer didn't always have a happy ending on earth. But like Cathy said, God works everything together for the good of those who love him. And if anybody loved God, Cathy did. One way or another, I believed everything would turn out okay.

ॐॐॐ

FOUND

That summer, a youth group from another part of the state came to hold a Vacation Bible School for the children at our church. Over the course of the week, many of us became friends with the people from that church — so much so that a group of us went to visit them in their town a few weeks later.

While I was there, I hit it off with a guy in his mid-30s named Sean.

"Hey, if you have a free day, do you want to ride around with me tomorrow while I make deliveries?"

I had nothing better to do, so I agreed.

"So, what do you want to do with your life?" Sean asked the next morning, turning to look at me in the passenger's seat of his truck.

"Oh, you know, whatever God wants."

But my cliché pat answer was not enough for Sean.

"What kinds of things do you do?"

"Well, I like sports."

He had to drag it out of me, but Sean eventually learned that I'd been a decent baseball player in high school, though I hadn't been given much playing time.

"I might know some people. Let me make some phone calls and see if I can get you into some college tryouts."

Whatever, I thought. I really didn't think anything would come of it.

But the following week, Sean called me.

"A coach at a Christian college in Greenville, South Carolina, wants to meet you," he said. "When can you come this way so I can take you down to meet him?"

SOMETHING GOOD

Everything happened very quickly after that. I threw with the baseball coach at North Greenville University, and he agreed to let me play for him. It took some financial finagling, some prayers and encouragement from both Sean and Cathy, but by the fall of 2000, I was living in South Carolina and attending college on a baseball scholarship. My life finally started to take some shape.

࿇࿇࿇

In 2001, while I was away at college, Cathy passed away. I was devastated. Cathy was like another mother to me and had done so much for me. Her entire life had been a force for *good*. As she neared the end of her cancer battle, Cathy had confided in me that she wasn't afraid to die and leave her daughter behind — mainly because she had seen firsthand the way God took care of me after my parents died. Witnessing how God provided everything I needed assured her that her daughter would be okay — that God would do the same for her. It was incredibly humbling for me to think that God used me and my situation to encourage such an amazing woman.

Having gotten a late start, I was an older college student. I was 25 when I was a senior, and my brother Paul and his wife constantly teased me about needing to settle down and find myself a wife. They even tried to set me up a few times, but I just wasn't interested. If I went on a date and even the slightest thing annoyed me about a girl, I'd just move on with the attitude that I didn't have time to deal with the drama. I didn't need that stuff in my life. Because of that, they called me shallow and difficult to please. But, really, I just didn't want to settle. I figured that if God wanted me to get married, he would bring the right girl to me when the time was right.

An old friend from my youth group back home attended the University of Tennessee, and even though our friendship was purely platonic, she was bent on visiting my roommate and me in Greenville for a weekend.

"Why would you want to come here?" I asked her, thinking she must be really bored.

"It'd be cool to check it out."

So Jenna came down to visit, and it was nice to spend time with an old friend. She and I weren't really each other's type, so our relationship would never progress beyond friendship. At the end of the weekend, she invited me to visit her sometime. I blew it off since I knew it'd be difficult to squeeze in a trip, but as the weeks passed, I felt guilty. I owed it to her to go check out Knoxville. I called her up.

"Okay, if I'm going to come see you — if I'm going to drive all the way up there — then I'm going to need you to set me up with a date," I joked.

It was a two-and-a-half-hour drive from Greenville to Knoxville, and I arrived about 11 p.m. on a Friday. Jenna was working but told me her roommate would let me in. Her roommate, however, was clearly annoyed by the situation. Marie usually went to bed early, but my visit obligated her to stay up late with me, the stranger planning to crash on the couch in the living room. She was really attractive, and I was interested in getting to know her, but I could tell she found me irritating. In my typical fashion, I decided to have a good time, anyway, whether or not I aggravated her. After all, I *was* on vacation. The next day, Jenna showed me all around Knoxville before breaking the news that she was ditching me for a hot date that night.

"Well, that's okay," I said, grinning. "I'd be glad to take your roommate out!"

Despite Marie's objections, I took her to a movie that evening. She refused to eat the popcorn I bought because then she'd have to admit that we were on a "date," and she wasn't about to admit that!

The next day, as we all attended the Tennessee baseball game as a group, I could tell I was grating on Marie's nerves, and I began to feel bad for some of the intentional teasing things I'd done to irritate her further. I decided I needed to distance myself from her and somehow try to leave on a positive note. Marie was really beautiful and seemed like a nice girl.

That afternoon, after Jenna left for work, I struck up a normal conversation with Marie in the apartment. We sat and talked for an hour until she began to see that there was more to me than what she'd seen earlier in the weekend. We were actually on the same page in a lot of areas, which was refreshing to me. She was a pleasant person with a wonderful personality. By the time I headed back to Greenville that evening, I felt like maybe I had salvaged the possibility for a friendship with her.

When Jenna wasn't looking, I got Marie's number out of her phone. We stayed in touch over the next few months while I graduated from college with my Business Administration degree. We talked on the phone every few days, and in July, I decided to go visit her again. I was beginning to think there might be more to this thing than friendship.

Two years later, I proposed, and by September 2006, we were married. I could not believe God had given me such a perfect partner for my life. I hadn't even been looking, and yet God knew exactly what I needed. Once again, he was working everything together for my good.

అ అ అ

Marie and I moseyed through the airport, hand-in-hand, pulling our carry-on bags on wheels behind us. Like most honeymooners, we were still riding on the high of our wedding and looking forward to spending a week alone together. For us, it would be a lovely Alaskan cruise.

We still had an hour until our plane departed for Seattle, so we arrived at our gate ready to relax for a bit, when we saw the flight to Seattle pulling away from the concourse.

"Wait. It's not time yet!" Marie frantically checked her plane ticket for the listed departure time. "See? We still have an hour!"

I marched up to the ticket counter, but the airline representative said nothing could be done. The plane had left. Nobody seemed to know why it departed earlier than scheduled. The airline helped re-route us via a flight to Houston, which would still get us to Seattle in time to board the cruise ship. But in Houston, we encountered a "rain delay," even though it was a perfectly sunny day with blue skies. It was beginning to seem like we weren't supposed to get on that ship.

"This is ridiculous." Marie sighed, as we sat in the Houston airport, calculating how much time we'd have to get from the airport to the dock after we landed.

But by the time we got to Seattle, it was too late. We'd chased our deadline across the country only to realize that our ship had literally sailed, and we hadn't even gotten to wave goodbye.

కచచచ

We tried to catch up with the cruise ship at the next port, but to no avail. Deciding to make the most of the hand we'd been dealt, we agreed to spend the week exploring Seattle since neither of us had been there before. We stayed with Marie's grandparents, whom I'd never met. Although they were very welcoming and accommodating, it felt more like a family vacation than a honeymoon.

After a week, we flew back to my hometown in North Carolina. But instead of getting to carry my bride over the threshold in a grand gesture and make up for some of the lost honeymoon romance, we were greeted by an overwhelming flea problem in the house. Feeling defeated, we dragged our suitcases into the pop-up camper still set up in the front yard for wedding guests and spent the next several days camping out.

Marie was naturally an optimistic person, but our rough start to marriage took its toll. I tried to keep things light and help her keep everything in perspective.

"Welcome to my life," I said wryly, wrapping my arms around her. "If it can go wrong, it will. The way I see it, God *must* have *great* plans for us. He allows these things so we can be challenged and grow."

"I guess so," she said, smiling.

We moved to Greenville, and Marie started her job, while I accepted a position as the athletic groundskeeper at my alma mater. We got an apartment and, through a series of events, somehow ended up with three dogs.

Things were just starting to fall into place when an accident completely totaled my truck. Then, late one night in March, someone started pounding on our apartment door. I ignored it for a while, thinking that no good could come of opening a door to someone at 10 p.m., especially somebody knocking as furiously as they were.

"Justin, get the door!" Marie yelled from the shower.

I opened the door and was hit immediately with a wall of smoke from the hallway.

"The building's on fire! Everyone, out!"

"Okay, thanks!" I shut the door to keep further smoke from entering our unit, then turned and walked calmly back to the bedroom, poking my head in the master bathroom.

"We've got to go," I stated, matter-of-factly.

"What? I'm in the shower!"

"It doesn't matter. There's a fire. We've gotta go."

Marie dressed quickly, and we exited through our sliding glass door onto the patio. But as we stood in the parking lot with the other tenants, we only counted two of our three dogs.

"Where's Fisher?" Marie asked, looking around. Fisher was known for being a friendly dog, always looking for food and people to pet him. "We've got to find him!"

Marie and I scoured the parking lot and other nearby areas for the next hour, while the fire department fought the fire in our building. He was nowhere to be found.

Finally, when the fire was out and the smoke had cleared, a firefighter found Fisher in the hallway outside our unit, covered in soot and passed out from smoke inhalation. He had apparently gone into the smoky hallway in the midst of the chaos. The vets did all they could, but Fisher ended up dying.

Although the fire did not touch our apartment directly, the building was considered unstable, and we were never allowed back inside. We could stand there and literally see our possessions just feet away, but the restoration team set up a safety barrier so that we couldn't go in. They pulled out a few of our things for us, but the majority of our stuff was damaged from smoke getting through the vents. We would have to start over.

FOUND

In the weeks that followed, Marie and I had many deep conversations in our hotel room, and we came to terms with the fact that life isn't easy — bad things happen, even to followers of Jesus. We had to accept it, all the while remembering that God was the one in ultimate control and that he had creative ways of working everything out. Like Peter walking on the water, we had to keep our eyes on Jesus and not let ourselves get distracted by the storm around us. I had found that in spite of the challenges and suffering I'd faced in my 27 years, I was still a happy person who enjoyed life.

I thought of my favorite scriptures again: "God works all things together for the good of those who love him" and "Seek the kingdom of God above all else … and he will give you everything you need."

As for the apartment, everything we lost were just "things." As for my wrecked truck, it was just a "thing." The honeymoon was just a trip. There would be others. Over the years, I learned to put things in perspective — to realize what was really worth worrying about. If God had been so good to take care of me after my parents died, then I was confident that he would continue to do so the rest of my life. A lot of our needs were relatively minor compared to the struggles I previously faced. And none of it was too big for God to handle.

Our church determined to do something to help us, so they talked Marie into going to Target and setting up our wedding registry all over again. And, through the goodness of our fellow believers, our belongings were replaced, one by one. True to his word, God gave us everything we needed.

෧෧෧

The years after that were quiet as Marie and I took advantage of our employee discount on tuition rates at the college to earn undergraduate and master's degrees, respectively. I even taught some business courses at the university after I graduated. We had some friends living in Travelers Rest, a picturesque, mountainous community north of Greenville, so we bought a house there and settled into a happy life. We attended a great, uplifting church nearby called Upcountry Church, where we continued to learn and grow in our faith.

Marie and I loved taking our dogs on hikes, and on one such excursion, as we wound our way through the trees toward a waterfall, we reminisced about our rough beginnings.

"Remember how your house was infested with fleas?" Marie flashed me her winning smile.

"Yes! We had to stay in that pop-up camper for a week!" I responded, realizing how grateful I was for our spacious, comfortable home.

"And that honeymoon — the race across the country so we could stay with distant relatives." Marie giggled.

I smiled to myself. We had been privileged to take some great trips since the infamous failed honeymoon.

There were actually many things like that in my life.

FOUND

My parents' deaths were horrible, but looking back, I now realized that if they hadn't died, a lot of other good things would not have happened. I wouldn't have seen firsthand how God provided everything my family needed, whether through the generosity of our church or the life insurance money. I wouldn't have seen the change in my brother Paul, who gave up his party lifestyle to rally around my siblings and me and keep us a close-knit family. I wouldn't have gotten to know Cathy, a true friend who prayed for me before we ever met, who challenged me to grow as a person and as a Christian. If I hadn't met Cathy and gotten involved in the church, I wouldn't have met Sean, who set the wheels in motion for my baseball scholarship and college education. And I also wouldn't have met my friend Jenna, through whom I met my beautiful wife, Marie.

Ultimately, if my parents had not passed away and I hadn't gone through the grief, suffering and resulting growth, I wasn't sure whether I would have become strong. I couldn't say whether or not I'd trade one life for the other. The point was that even when I didn't see any way for a situation in my life to be anything other than tragic, somehow God worked it out. Of course, I didn't believe he was responsible for my parents' deaths, but he certainly didn't waste any time in, ever so creatively, getting my life back on track.

I didn't serve God because he promised good things to happen to me. I served him because he loved me. I served him because of his son, Jesus, who rescued me from the possibility of hell and from my own personal doom. The bad things I'd experienced caused my faith and trust in God to grow, because he was there for me when nobody else was. And since my focus was on him, everything eventually fell into place.

"You know, I've always known God works everything out for good," I mused. "I don't always understand how or why, but every step of my life has led to the next one without me having to force anything. God has always revealed the next thing he wants me to do right when he wants me to do it."

"Like your baseball scholarship," Marie reminded me. "That was definitely God intervening and making sure you went to college, and you didn't even see it coming."

"Right! And like you — I wasn't looking for a wife, but God knew I needed you."

Marie pushed her sunglasses to her forehead, and her eyes met mine in a loving glance. We had reached the waterfall at last, and the noise of the rushing water would make further conversation difficult. We both gazed at the wall of water cascading off the cliff above and tumbling over the rocks below.

If God had taken care of me to that point, I knew the rest of my life would be no different.

As long as I put him first, I believed that everything — even the most devastating situations — could be turned around in an instant into something undeniably, unbelievably good.

STRENGTH TO FORGIVE
The Story of Annette
Written by Ameerah Collins

"You don't have anything to worry about. I've walked many young girls, just like you, through this exact procedure."

The blond counselor sat before me with clasped hands and crossed legs. She was so graceful, so poised and perfect. Her ruby lips uttered soft, caring and seemingly comforting words that crowded my head. Deep in my heart, I knew she wasn't telling me the whole truth. Still, I wanted to believe her — I *needed* to believe her.

"Annette." The woman clicked her long nails on the mahogany desk and smiled at me. "Those feelings are totally normal, however, they are unnecessary. You must remember it's not really a baby. It's just tissue and cells."

I bowed my head. My heart ached terribly. I sighed. I felt shame. If the pain of my decision was so intense before the procedure, how would it be afterward?

You know she's lying, I told myself. *This is something she does every day. She probably has her lines rehearsed and all.*

"Perhaps it'll make you feel better if I show you pictures of what's in your stomach, yes?" The woman laid out several photos. "See, embryos curved into c-shapes with translucent skin. It's just a tiny blob of tissue. Didn't I tell you?"

FOUND

I traced my hands over the pictures. "A blob of tissue? Not a baby? No heartbeat?"

"Of course, Annette." She gathered the photos and shoved them back in her desk. "You're having this abortion as early as possible. The embryo won't feel any pain. You're making the right choice."

The right choice. Those words troubled me. My mind pushed me to agree — to fully accept her words and cease my distress. *Not a baby. No heartbeat. Just a blob of tissue. But if that's true, why do I feel so guilty?*

༽༽༽

Throughout my early childhood, our family loved one another, and our home was happy. My parents raised my two brothers and me in church, and we never missed a Sunday.

Mom and Dad were pretty active church members, too, and everyone looked up to them as if they were the epitome of a happily married couple. They never argued, fussed or glared at each other in disdain. So imagine my surprise at 7 years old when my parents announced their divorce.

Over the next year, my father gradually exited our lives. Living so close to him was too much for Mom to bear. She needed a fresh start. So, when I was 8, Mom uprooted my brothers and me and took us to Florida.

She kept us in church, though. That never changed. Eventually, Mom met a man named Ralph. They married when I was 11 years old. Though Dad's desertion shocked me and left me broken, part of me felt, or perhaps hoped, that Ralph wouldn't leave us. I wanted him to take my brothers and me under his wing and treat us as his own blood. To be in it for the long haul. Thankfully, Ralph didn't disappoint.

When I turned 15, Mom and Ralph moved our family to Tennessee. I hated leaving Florida. I'd become used to the beautiful weather, diverse cultures and unending entertainment, as well as the huge church we attended. I didn't want to leave my friends behind. The thought of trying to fit in at a new school, church and neighborhood frightened me.

I made friends, but they were different from my churchgoing friends in Florida. My new friends were a pleasant bunch, who just liked to hang out and have fun. They had boyfriends and attended the occasional party with alcohol present, but they weren't wild party animals. However, they weren't raised in a Christian home like me, and that's what truly made the difference. They didn't bother with church, and I believed if I made church a priority then I'd lose them. I sought their total acceptance, and if that meant cutting off some of my "good girl" ways, then so be it.

There were no other girls my age at church, and it seemed boring. But I kept going to church, only because Mom and Ralph made me. Later, I started dating Adam, a boy two years my senior. Slowly, the teachings and influence of my parents began to fade. Although I didn't necessarily dislike church, my desire to hang out with my friends and boyfriend trumped my desire to attend church. I had fun with them, but part of me felt guilty for putting my friendships and relationship before God. But I believed if I made church a priority then I'd lose my friends and Adam.

Two years later, Adam prepared to leave for college, and we began sleeping together. I felt guilty for doing something I'd been taught not to do until marriage. But I wanted to please Adam. I dreamed we would marry someday and ride off into the sunset, like the happy ending of a fairytale, and I did everything in my power to keep Adam around and win his approval.

But once Adam became a college boy, he had no use for a high school girl like me.

࿓࿓࿓

When I started college, it was the ultimate escape from my parents' rules. In their household, I enjoyed limited freedom. Or so I thought. I'd been yearning for freedom throughout high school. Freshman year of college, I started drinking, hanging out late with my new friends and smoking pot. I wasn't a crazy drunk who passed out on strangers' lawns or danced on tabletops, I was just a social drinker with no desire to get completely wasted.

Soon, I began dating James. He grew up Catholic but only attended church a couple times a year. That was perfect, I thought. Although I still possessed much love for the people at my church, I knew my lifestyle wasn't aligned with the Christian life. So I placed church on the back burner. I just wanted to hang out with my friends and fall deeper in love with James.

After dating for a while, James and I started sleeping together. Being with him made me feel alive, giddy and carefree. We couldn't get enough of each other.

James and I discussed marriage after graduation, so when I discovered my pregnancy, I assumed our desire to build our lives together wouldn't change. One night he stopped by to see me at my parents' house when they weren't home, and I just came out and told him. No hesitation. No stalling. Just truth.

"James." I looked at him beside me, nestled together on my family's living room sofa. "I'm pregnant."

"What?" James turned toward me and clasped his large palms around my hands. "You can't be pregnant, Annette. How did this happen?"

"What do you mean how did this happen? We had unprotected sex, James."

"I should have been more responsible." James swore. "I can't have a kid, Annette. Heck, *you* can't have a kid. Your parents would freak!"

"You think I'm not scared to face them? You have no idea how scared I've been since I found out. My parents will look at me so differently. I don't even want them to know, but that's impossible. Once I start showing, it won't take a genius to realize what's up."

"I don't want to involve our parents just yet," James

said. "I'm not ready to be a father, and you aren't ready to be a mother. We have our whole lives ahead of us."

"It's a big commitment, I know, but —"

"It's a *colossal* commitment. We still have to finish college. I mean, c'mon, Annette, we're just a couple of broke college kids. We have to think about our education, careers and future. We can't have a kid. It's crazy!"

"I know it's crazy, James!" I shrieked. "You think I haven't thought about all that?" I tore my hands from his. A burst of anger ripped through me. "Didn't we talk about marriage, though? You said if this happened we'd get married, but now you're acting like we never discussed having a life together at all."

"I'm just being real, Annette." He stood and paced the carpet while I sat there, looking up at him, completely bewildered. "We're talking about a whole other life that has to be supported. I need to think about what we're going to do about our problem. We need to really weigh our options — figure a way out."

"Our baby isn't the problem. What *we* did is the problem. *We* brought this on ourselves. The life inside of me didn't ask for careless parents."

James flopped down beside me and closed his eyes. "I'm sorry. I didn't mean it like that. I know we screwed up. I just ..." His eyes opened and met mine. "I can't financially support you and a child right now. The best solution would be to end this without our parents finding out."

"What are you saying?"

"You know what I'm saying, Annette."

"I can't." I gritted my teeth, willing the tears to stay hidden. "I can't take the life of my own child. My mother didn't raise me that way. I can't just do that, James."

"Annette," he said. Sorrow clouded his eyes, and he briefly bowed his head. He sniffed and cleared his throat, looking at me with determination. "We need you to get an abortion. It's the only way out. Your parents won't find out, and neither will my mom."

"Kill our baby?" My voice trembled. My eyes blurred with unshed tears.

"Don't say it like that."

"But it is that." The dam I tried to restrain finally broke. Tears, cloaked in mascara, slid down my face. A rush of weakness abruptly overcame me, and I slumped over. I buried my head in my lap and clutched my belly.

I felt overwhelmed, lost, afraid. I wanted my parents to continue seeing me as their good college daughter, not their pregnant teenager. I couldn't risk the possibility of James leaving me or growing to hate me if I decided to keep the baby.

So, I nodded, giving in to what I supposed was best.

The following days, I moved through campus like a zombie. Nothing seemed to matter. I tried to focus on schoolwork, but my plans to have an abortion kept my eyes leaking with despair.

Days later, James and I attended a consultation at an abortion clinic. The counselor exuded elegance and sophistication.

FOUND

Why have such a pretty person in such an ugly place?

I instantly knew the answer.

Her kind smile was meant to soothe my worries and alleviate my concerns, but part of me saw it as a devious leer. She defined abortion as a safe and harmless procedure to rid women of an unplanned circumstance. Who was it safe and harmless for exactly? Just me? She said it was just a blob of tissue. I wanted so desperately to accept her words as truth and just get the abortion over with. So, I forced myself to really listen. To stop myself from asking harder questions. I wanted to give in.

Slowly, I began to believe her words. Her definition of abortion seemed much easier to swallow than my own. I wanted to get rid of the ache. I needed to eliminate that gut feeling telling me not to sign any papers or schedule a date for the procedure. My heart raged in my chest, beating against the ribs caging it and pushing me to speak up. But my voice was lost. Gone with the teachings of my childhood. Gone with my morals. Just gone.

The day of my procedure, I woke up feeling dirty. Like I was about to commit a heinous crime. I covered myself in pear-scented lotion, hoping to mask how unclean I felt. It didn't help.

When James arrived to pick me up from my parents' home, we argued before we could even leave my room, shouting and screaming at one another over what we were about to do. "We're making the wrong choice."

"It's not wrong. It's the best choice for us. I thought we went over this." James sighed.

"We did, but I think we're being rash, James. We're not the first teenagers to screw up like this. Maybe we can talk to someone — someone who will guide us in the right direction."

"Talk to who?" His voice heightened with incredulity. "Whoever we talk to, your folks *will* find out. Do you want that to happen?"

"No." I glanced down at my tightened fists, hating the whimper in my voice. "I'm just afraid we're making a huge mistake. It's not just termination of a pregnancy. We're taking a life — our *baby's* life."

"Jesus, *Annette!* Seriously? You pick now to have this conversation?" He ran his hands through his hair, knotting it in curls. Months before, I would have ached to smooth his hair back. But in that moment, I couldn't stand to be near him. "You heard the counselor at the clinic. It's not a baby — heck, it's not even a fetus — so stop calling it that! It's tissue and cells."

"Every time I'm close to accepting that —" My voice cracked. I slumped onto my mattress, mainly to disguise my wobbling knees. "Something tells me not to. It doesn't matter if it isn't a 'baby' or a 'fetus.' I think it's a life."

He massaged his temples. "I cannot believe you're saying this. We can't just back out. If you have this baby, you'll have to drop out of school and take care of it. Are you ready to put your entire life on hold, Annette? Are you ready for everyone to know about this? Because I'm not."

I halted. A burdening silence surrounded us. It

stretched out between us, wider and wider, creating a distance I'd never felt with James before. My heart pounded as I studied his face. I was so afraid.

"I don't know," I whispered.

James hung his head — like he'd lost a battle. He left without a word, leaving me to wrestle with my thoughts. I had so much to consider. I didn't want to see the disapproval and shock on my mother's face when I broke the news of my pregnancy. I shivered at the thought of wobbling to class with a protruding belly, the professors and students giving me a judgmental side-eye. And James … I couldn't force fatherhood on him.

James didn't stay gone long. Minutes later, he knocked at the door, and I answered. He stood on the porch with hunched shoulders and his hands shoved in his pockets. That same loud silence returned, probing at my skin like needles and thorns. He stared at me, desperation in his eyes.

Silently, we agreed that this was the best decision for both of us. I grabbed my purse and walked out the door as James followed close behind.

James and I were led into a waiting room with several other couples. I practically dragged my feet to a chair, feeling like dead weight. The room had peach walls and light-colored flooring. It looked homelike, but it was cold, and my skin felt clammy. After waiting for a while, I was escorted to a small room with a television to watch a video to further prepare me for the abortion procedure. The video explained the feelings and emotions that couples, especially women, may experience after abortion. The narrator had such a soft and calming voice, just like my counselor.

"You may feel sad or grieved for a short period of time, but afterward, you'll be just fine," the narrator said. Photos of dejected-looking women raced across the screen before being replaced with the same women appearing cheerful and liberated. "These feelings do not last long. You can expect to be your normal self again, very soon. You'll feel relieved, refreshed and content with your choice."

It can't be that easy, I thought. *Should I believe this?*

After the video, I went back to the waiting area with James until a nurse called me back once more. She placed me in a tiny changing room with a curtain and handed me a gown to change into. I stood there, waiting my turn. I felt nauseous. I thought about putting my clothes back on and running out the door, but my legs wouldn't move. Guilt started to seep through my pores and oozed over every inch of my skin.

"Annette." A plump little nurse with rosy cheeks peeked in through the curtain and offered me a kind smile. "We're ready for you, dear."

The nurse led me to yet another room and instructed me to lie down on the exam table. I closed my eyes as they readied me. They placed my legs in stirrups, softly speaking to one another.

"Are you sure you want to go through with this, honey?" the same nurse asked me.

"Yes." *Maybe not.*

"You can always change your mind; it's not too late."

"I'm sure." *No, I'm not. Maybe I should leave.*

But I did it, anyway. As the procedure began, I begged God to forgive me. The guilt and shame was so heavy — like a bag of stones pressed upon my chest.

When I walked out of the room, I wanted to drop to the floor and bury myself in the ground, but a nurse took me to a recovery room. It looked so comfortable — recliner chairs were situated in a large circle. Other ladies and teenagers who'd just undergone abortions sat in the room, too. They appeared fine, but I wondered if that was just a front. Did they wear a mask like me? Did they hide the pain gutting their insides?

Later, a male counselor took me to a private room where James sat waiting for me. The counselor asked me a series of follow-up questions. They wanted to make sure I didn't have any negative emotions about the abortion.

"Do you have any suicidal thoughts at this time?" the man asked.

"No." *I just killed my baby. I should be dead, too.*

"Are you depressed, Annette?"

"I think I'm fine." *But why is there a growing hole in my heart?*

"Do you feel guilty about this decision? Or do you feel relief?"

"I'm relieved, I think. I'm fine." *I've made a mistake. God, what have I done?*

"Okay!" he said, smiling.

STRENGTH TO FORGIVE

❧❧❧

Soon after the abortion, I received a packet in the mail from the clinic. It was a follow-up packet about my abortion. I should have crumbled it up and thrown it in the trash, but I slipped it in my desk drawer. Not long after, my mother found the packet.

"Annette!" Mom called me, and I ran toward her voice. She stood in my room with the thick packet in her shaking hands. "Is this what I think it is? Did you have an abortion?"

I stood there with my mouth open. I couldn't believe Mom found out. One of the main reasons for getting the abortion was so she and Ralph would never find out about my pregnancy. All I could do was nod my head. My shoulders slumped as she sat down on my bed and bowed her head. I could practically see the fury and disappointment racing through her mind. I slid down the wall and onto the floor, burying my head in my lap.

"Do you hate me?" I asked her through my broken sobs.

"No, I could never hate you, Annette. You're my child." Mom walked over to me and sat beside me against the wall. "I wish you would have talked to me. I wish you could have trusted me enough to come to me with this."

"It wasn't that, Mom." I tugged my knees up to my chest and wrapped my arms around my legs, hugging myself. "I just didn't want to disappoint you. I felt so horrible and dirty — no, I *feel* so horrible and dirty. I wish

I'd never done it. I tried to convince myself that it wasn't really a baby. But, really, I killed my baby. And there's no taking it back."

"We're going to get through this." Mom's voice trembled, and I turned my head to peer at her. Tears slid down her face. She was so hurt. "If this ever happens again, come to me. We can discuss you keeping the baby or giving it up for adoption. But never abortion, Annette. Never abortion."

Mom said she felt compelled to enter my room and look in my desk. At first I wondered why she invaded my privacy, but now I believe it was God giving me an opportunity to confide in my mom about the decision I'd made. In the days leading up to my abortion, I focused my attention on avoiding Mom and Ralph's disappointment. I didn't want them to see me differently. I'd forgotten how loving and caring my parents were, but God didn't forget. I believe he knew my pain, and he knew Mom could help me.

The semester after the abortion, I transferred to a state college. There, I turned to alcohol and weed. The drugs and alcohol numbed my pain. Each high halted my feelings of regret, shame and hurt. James struggled over our decision, too, and started drinking his sorrows away. While drunk, he apologized for pushing me into making that choice. I tried to tell him it wasn't solely his fault. I could have walked out of that abortion clinic, but I didn't. He beat himself up, though, calling himself a coward.

I hated myself. I constantly asked why I didn't fight

harder to protect what I truly believed to be a human life. Why didn't I talk to my parents? Why didn't I return to church and talk to my pastor's wife? The adults in my life could have shed light on my situation. Maybe things would have turned out differently. Perhaps they would have encouraged me to make a better choice — *the right choice.*

ঙ্কঙ্কঙ্ক

It wasn't long before I got pregnant again. James and I weren't willing to seek another abortion, but it didn't make telling my parents any easier. When I told Mom and Ralph, they weren't surprised. Ralph was stern yet loving with me. He and Mom would help as much as possible, but I had to remember the child was my responsibility. Relying on my parents to do everything for this baby was out of the question. My parents even discussed marriage with us, but James decided against that. Gradually, we went from being a loving couple to becoming a hazard to one another. We eventually broke up. The abortion drove a wedge between us — we weren't the same anymore. Co-parenting would be enough.

After my college semester ended, I moved back in with my parents. I stopped drinking and smoking when I found out I was pregnant and even started going to church again. Though I didn't go regularly, I knew I needed to. There was a tugging in my heart, telling me I'd been away from God for way too long. I tried to ignore it, but I couldn't.

FOUND

Going through my second pregnancy was difficult. Feeling the heartbeat of my child and seeing her through the ultrasound reminded me of how I'd ended the life of my first child. I knew this time that what was growing inside of me wasn't just a bunch of cells like the counselor from the abortion clinic said. There was an actual baby going through various stages of development. I was happy for the birth of this child, but I couldn't get over the death of my first.

A friend of mine from high school, Bryce, helped me throughout the pregnancy. He didn't expect anything from me, he was just a shoulder to lean on. Anytime I wanted to hang out, he was there. If I needed to talk or cry, he let me.

Months later, I gave birth to Ariel. I laid in the hospital bed, gazing down at my little baby girl wrapped in a white hospital blanket. Ariel was so perfect — so beautiful, pure and innocent. How could I have given up her older brother or sister? I held her close to my chest as tears escaped my eyes and landed on her small forehead. I gently wiped them away, but my sobs deepened at the touch of her soft skin.

A heavy sorrow rested upon me. I was so happy looking at Ariel, but I was so grieved thinking about the little one I'd thrown away. I felt broken. Right then, I knew I hadn't just hurt the baby I'd aborted or caused pain just for myself. I'd hurt the heart of God.

I'd loved church as a child. I'd loved learning all about God. And even though I believed he loved me and wanted me close, I left the church and pulled away from him. I went my own way with a head full of memorized verses from the Bible, but no true relationship with Jesus.

For so many years, I hadn't given much thought to how God gave his son, Jesus, to die for me. I didn't think about the sacrifice Jesus made so I could be with him in heaven one day. God allowed his son to endure beatings, ridicule, torture and hurt. He did that for me and the entire world. God sacrificed his son for me. But I gave my child up for nothing. How could I do that?

I broke down and cried. I begged God to forgive me for the abortion, for killing the life he was in the midst of creating.

God, I know I'm not worthy to come to you with such a huge request. But I can't carry this burden anymore. I know that I made a mistake. Please, please forgive me.

It was almost as if he whispered to me, *I know that you're sorry. I love you more than you'll ever know. Annette, I forgive you.*

In that moment, I felt like God was near me in the hospital room — embracing me and holding me while I wept with a sleeping Ariel in my arms. I didn't deserve his love. I didn't deserve to feel his overwhelmingly loving presence. That night, I surrendered my life to Jesus. I truly believe he forgave me for ending the life of my child.

ॐॐॐ

FOUND

Over the years, Bryce became my closest friend and confidant. My irregular trips to my parents' church steadily became regular again. I graduated from college, started a new job and forced myself to concentrate on my relationship with God, my family and my career.

One night in prayer, I told God, "I know you have someone out there for me who will be a wonderful stepdad to Ariel, and I am going to trust your timing."

As I trusted God with that, my friendship with Bryce developed beyond friendship. When Ariel was 3 years old, Bryce and I got married. I found it amazing how I'd already known my soul mate for years. I just needed God to help point him out to me.

Bryce and I made serious lifestyle changes. We made it a point to go to church, to pray together and read the Bible. We let go of friends who weren't the best influences in our lives. Bryce and I wanted to get closer to God — to learn more about him and please him with our lives.

Having Bryce in my life was wonderful.

We became accountability partners to one another, constantly challenging the other to be better and to do good for others.

❧❧❧

Bryce and I had more children. However, during every pregnancy, the guilt of my abortion crawled back to burden me with shame. My unwillingness to forgive myself affected the way I treated my husband and my children. I felt like I didn't deserve to have them in my life.

STRENGTH TO FORGIVE

Why did God bless me with more wonderful children when I'd chosen to end the life of my first baby? How could a woman like me deserve someone as loving and understanding as Bryce?

Feelings of hatred and shame piled up over the years. But after a while I grew tired of the sadness ailing me. In 2009, a woman at my church in Tennessee held a Bible study group geared toward abortion recovery. Sheila's Bible study aimed to help men and women reclaim their peace of mind, discover their self-worth and experience how far God's love and forgiveness truly extends. I wanted to attend one of the studies, but I was afraid of what people at church would think of me.

During a women's retreat at church, a woman from Sheila's abortion recovery Bible study spoke about her experience. Selene talked about how she suffered from guilt and struggled with shame for many years.

"Jesus offers forgiveness and healing for the things that haunt us," she said, "and when we express our sorrow to him and ask for forgiveness, he gives it to us." It was as if she was speaking right to me. I was astounded by how similar her experience was to mine. After her speech, I pulled Selene to the side and talked to her about my abortion.

"I don't really talk about it," I told her. "It's a time in my life that I wish I could forget. But I was just wondering about what you said up there. I've asked Jesus to forgive me, and I know he has, but I can't bear to forgive myself. How did you do that?"

FOUND

Selene nodded in understanding. "God loves us, Annette. I believe that he has truly forgiven you and me because we've asked him to. You and I have to allow ourselves to accept that fully. When I asked God to forgive me, it wasn't long before he gave me the courage to forgive myself."

"But forgiving myself seems wrong. God is supposed to forgive me. I mean," I said, smiling, "he's our big and powerful God. He's capable of anything. But how can I forgive myself for such a horrible act? I believe I should suffer — like I deserve this ache."

"Annette, Jesus died to free us from the guilt we feel from the poor choices we make." Selene hugged me, but I'm sure she could still detect how conflicted I was. "God has forgiven you. He'll give you the strength to forgive yourself."

After that conversation, I began praying every night and asking God to help me forgive myself. I thought about the day Mom found the packet and she said she was disappointed and upset with the choice I had made, but she still loved me.

I believed my choice to be unforgiveable, but Mom forgave me, anyway. Often, I felt God reminding me, *Annette. I love you. How many times do I have to tell you I forgive you? I'm your father. Your decision disappointed me, but I still love you. My love for you will never change.*

With God's help, I knew I could learn to let go.

A little more than a year after the women's retreat, I decided I would ask Sheila at church about the abortion recovery Bible study. Though I would always long for the baby I lost, I knew it was time to ease the burden I'd been carrying with me for more than a decade.

I texted Sheila and asked when the next recovery group would be.

Sheila responded, "Oh, do you have a friend?"

"No. It's for me."

The next Sunday, I talked to Sheila about it.

"This has been on my heart for a while, and I believe God wants me to attend the Bible study."

"Oh, Annette!" she said. "I am so surprised! I've known you for years and had no idea."

"I know. I've been contemplating coming to the study, but I just felt so ashamed. I've wondered what others will think of me. How my reputation will change. But now I just don't care. I want to be able to speak openly about my experience and encourage other young girls not to make the same mistake I made. I think the study will help me."

"Well, I think so, too!" Sheila smiled.

❧❧❧

A few months later, I attended my first abortion recovery Bible study. It was held in a small room in our church.

The atmosphere was very confidential and respectful. Though the women didn't judge one another, the class was extremely difficult.

On my first visit, Sheila asked us to share our abortion

experience if we felt comfortable. There were only about seven or eight other women present with similar stories, but I still felt so vulnerable. I'd buried my hate, shame and guilt for so long that retelling my abortion experience was the most challenging feat I ever had to accomplish.

But it helped.

Bringing such a dark part of my past to the light served as my first step to truly recovering and being able to speak about it.

Throughout the study, Sheila taught us to develop a deep connection with our lost child, no matter the circumstances surrounding our abortion. It was okay to mourn the loss of our child as if we'd actually given birth. I knew Jesus would always love me despite my wrongdoings, but the class helped me love myself again.

That same year, our family moved to South Carolina. We joined Upcountry Church. It's a very family-oriented church where everyone loves to love on one another. Though my church in Tennessee helped me face my abortion and forgive myself, Upcountry Church helped empower and equip me to tell my story.

I still wonder what my little one's personality would be like. I think of how he or she may have been a protective older sibling. I smile and cry, imagining the child's mannerisms. Who would he or she look like? I don't know, but I'm happy and confident that I'll see my child in heaven. How loving God is — I fully believe he will allow me to spend eternity with the child who died because of my own decision.

STRENGTH TO FORGIVE

Though I do not deserve his love and forgiveness, I do believe I have it.

Believing has set me free.

For more information about local chapters and resources for healing after an abortion, visit www.saveone.org.

TRUTH ON A TREADMILL
The Story of Rob Rucci
Written by Douglas Abbott

Something had gone wrong with the machine. I flailed my arms and tried to get to my feet, but it threw me around like an oversized doll. Designed to stop in the event of a fall, the track kept turning, and I wondered what kind of injuries might result. *What if it didn't stop at all? What if no one showed up to shut the thing off?*

While running on a treadmill pushed clear into the corner of my basement, my foot connected with the wall, causing me to tumble. The track flipped me end over end. Even as I thrashed around and my head connected painfully with the wall, I saw my life with utter clarity: I was a stubborn man, living for himself. I'd known for a long time what I ought to do, but I'd deliberately chosen otherwise.

The track turned and turned, and I thought, *This is the strangest lesson I have ever learned.*

❧ ❧ ❧

I grew up on a farm surrounded by thick hardwood forest. From early on, my brothers and I got up well before dawn and made our rounds on the farm. We tended dozens of pigs, rabbits and chickens and weeded and harvested a large vegetable garden. The small farm fed us abundantly and brought our family a small income as well.

My parents were strong as steel. My father worked an office job 40-plus hours each week, then worked through his weekends on the farm. I don't remember him taking a day off for any reason. Mom didn't, either. There was too much work to be done caring for five boys and a thriving farm.

My brothers and I received no allowance, so we kept traps in the outlying areas around the farm and sold the hides of the animals we caught to supply us with spending money. However, we found precious little time to spend it — our days were packed with farm chores, school, homework and more farm chores in the evening. Bedtime never had to be enforced.

Dad taught us to be respectful. He expressed his love in discipline and unwavering order. His legendary work ethic formed his single greatest contribution to my early identity.

"You're a smart boy, Rob. Strong for your age, too. You can do anything you set your mind to. Don't ever give anything less than your best."

Dad's convictions made an impact on all of us, mainly because he lived them. I relished the time I got to spend with him, scarce as it was with his constant work.

When my brothers and I needed gentle speech and reassurance, we went to Mom, a fount of affection with less-stringent requirements.

"It's up to you what you want to do with your life. Just

be happy." Mom seemed to have a built-in well of joy inside her. She was always amenable to sweeping me up into her arms for a hug and a flurry of kisses. However, she never left any confusion about the fact that "being happy" included hard work and good conduct. Mom grew up on a remote tract of land and rode horses bareback. She butchered animals alongside us. When an errant snake wound up in the house, Mom reached up into the rafters almost offhandedly to grab it and take it out to the woods.

My brothers and I fought like brothers often do, as we contended for space and self-respect, resulting in plenty of stitches, broken bones and visits to the hospital in those days. Our screen door required replacement more than once after adolescent bodies sailed through it in the heat of combat. I guess disagreements were inevitable among so many strong males in an environment that repelled weakness and anything un-masculine.

❧❧❧

Mom started bringing us to church when I was 6. Up to that time, my life pivoted on two main goals: pleasing my father and someday becoming a successful musician. I discovered early on that I had a good singing voice and a natural ability to play musical instruments. The worship leader at our church made use of my talents during the worship times on Sundays as I grew more proficient in singing and playing. In the meantime, I began to be interested in spiritual matters.

FOUND

Over the next few years, I listened carefully to the lessons in my Sunday school class, and one morning when our teacher invited us to pray and accept Christ, I eagerly accepted. If he made the world, he had the right to make the rules, and I was more than happy to follow them. I didn't need a great deal of adjustment in this area. I was already a hardworking, well-behaved child. I loved my parents and understood the importance of proper conduct — my father had seen to that with a firm resolve that never faltered. Now I began to get a glimpse of an invisible Father, much stronger and wiser than Dad, possessing a warmth and kindness toward his human children that captured my heart. I was loved and accepted and not only because I did my chores and got As and Bs on my report card. The Gospel message made perfect sense to me. In my mind, the only sensible response to the story of what happened on the cross was to love and trust the God who made me. He sent his son, Jesus, into the world to suffer and die so I could live. I was in.

❧❧❧

One morning, I went to church with Mom and my brothers for a regular Sunday service. A traveling evangelist gave the sermon. While I spent the service in children's church, Mom and my older brothers sat in the pews and listened to the sermon. Halfway through the message, the evangelist looked directly at Mom.

"Ma'am — yes, in the orange sundress there — do you have a boy in children's church this morning?"

"Yes, I do." Mom nodded.

"May I speak to you and your son after the service? I have a message for him."

"Okay," Mom called from the pew.

After the service, Mom retrieved me from the back of the church and brought me out into the hallway, where the evangelist stood socializing with other members as he waited for us.

He turned toward me with eyes that appeared strangely bright. "Rob, I was preaching a while ago and felt the Lord had a message for me to give to you. You're going to travel great distances when you get older. You will write songs about the Gospel and encourage many people in ways that will often involve music."

His words astonished me. The man standing in front of me was a complete stranger to us and to most of our church members as well. Nevertheless, he described the biggest dream in my 12-year-old heart — one I hadn't shared at length with anyone.

The evangelist's message never left me.

ॐॐॐ

I worked hard in school and went out for sports as well. As an extrovert, I enjoyed popularity that delighted me as a high school freshman. Musical success came just as easily to me, even in the competitive environment of the huge high school I attended in Raleigh.

By my junior year, my peers in the school band

selected my composition for the senior class song. That meant I got to sing at the graduation ceremony, a rarity for a junior. The next year, I played a different song that I wrote at my own graduation and was voted "Most Talented" along with another close friend and co-writer, who shared my passion for music.

My ego grew the most during those years. I not only became arrogant, I began to rebel against any form of authority. At the time, I didn't see it as disrespectful. I considered it my due.

Everything clicked for me — grades, opportunities, popularity and status. I played in a rock band and grew my hair halfway down my back. I came and went on a cruiser-styled motorcycle. Only my Christian convictions kept me from becoming a real troublemaker.

ॐॐॐ

My brothers all moved out on their own as soon as they could. Because of their examples and my own longing for independence, my departure from home happened quickly. I resumed playing bass guitar and singing lead with my old band, Introspect. Among my band mates were two of my brothers. The five of us took jobs, rented an old farmhouse and resolved to break into the music business with our own brand of hard Christian rock.

The next year, I reveled in my freedom and found plenty to enjoy about being a member of a rock band. Pretty girls and admirers flocked to the concerts we played. During that year, we gained a local following playing at churches and festivals. We even got to open several times for Whitecross — an immensely popular Christian metal band.

However, I began to see that my life was going nowhere. I played in a band without a record deal, while suffering through the grind of working menial jobs and watching my money evaporate each month. The hardship contrasted sharply with my big plans.

෨෨෨

"I need to come home." I sat on the very edge of Mom and Dad's sofa. My parents never showed me anything but love and generosity, but I felt sheepish sitting in their living room. I'd left with lofty plans and the air of one moving to a better neighborhood. But I'd scarcely been able to feed myself.

"Of course you can come home," they said, almost in unison. Mom smiled, and I saw compassion in her eyes.

"My plan is to go to college. I would appreciate all the help you can give me."

Dad helped me get accepted to a small college in Northeast Georgia, and I plunged into my studies. I cut off my rocker's hair and waded into academia with a vengeance. In my first year alone, I became an academic marshal, was voted in as vice president of my class and made the dean's list both semesters.

Two years after I began, I graduated with an associate's

degree in business administration and moved to Greenville, South Carolina, where I eventually continued my education and career. Early on, while I visited the area, a friend introduced me to one of the patrolmen at the sheriff's office of Pickens County. He was an older man who had served in law enforcement his whole life and had a truckload of stories to tell.

"I'll tell you something," he said, as we sat at an outdoor table sipping coffee. "Law enforcement isn't about being a tough guy." His eyebrows went up briefly. "It's not even completely about law and order. It's about people." He then told me amazing stories about people he helped and bizarre situations he encountered. I realized as we talked that this man was a *minister*, as much as if he'd been a preacher or an evangelist.

Based on that chance meeting, I applied for a position with the sheriff's office and within a few weeks started working as a 911 dispatcher. The job changed my life. I became intensely aware of the degree and pervasiveness of human suffering.

Many times, I was able to help coordinate life-saving resources and avert disaster. Other times, I was not.

One morning as I sat at the switchboard, a caller reported seeing a man turn his car off the road and drive straight into a telephone pole. The snapped pole fell over and crushed the car with the man inside it. Minutes later, a distraught young woman called and reported having a terrible fight with her husband, who'd left abruptly.

"He told me he was going to drive his car into a

telephone pole and kill himself," she sobbed into the phone. "I think he might actually do it." Police responders confirmed it was the same man. Because I was fielding the calls, it fell to me to connect the officers on the scene to the woman on the phone. It remains one of the most horrific experiences I participated in while fielding calls.

After a year of working 911 dispatch, the sheriff's office made me a deputy sheriff. There are a hundred crazy stories I could tell about that four-year gig. Every call brought me in contact with a unique mixture of personalities and circumstances. The frailty of humanity constantly surprised me. I encountered people derailed by alcoholism and addiction, divorce, premature death, betrayal and financial collapse. I looked into people's eyes and saw the entire spectrum of human emotions. I bore a huge weight, knowing that in some situations I might be the only thing standing in the way of catastrophe for the people I was trying to help.

My time as a deputy sheriff humbled me and taught me to rely on God. Many days, I drove criminal suspects to be booked at the jail. I often talked with them during the drive. When they were receptive, I shared my faith with them. One young man prayed with me as he sat on his handcuffs behind the safety glass, tears coursing down his cheeks. When I turned him over to the jailer, I jotted down the number of the police chaplain and told him I would be praying for him. Later, I learned that upon his release from prison, he joined a local church and reformed himself.

FOUND

My experience in law enforcement deepened my relationship with God. Seeing and dealing with human despair and cruelty every day enforced what I already believed — Jesus died to save us, in spite of ourselves.

❧❧❧

My first church home in the Greenville area was a thriving fellowship with plenty of college students. I noticed one young member immediately — Mary Beth had large hazel eyes and long brown hair. She was beautiful.

Over the next year, as I warmed to the church and got involved in its ministries and groups, I kept running into Mary Beth.

"I'm not interested in dating casually," I told her as we shared pie and coffee on our first date. "I'm looking for my future spouse." I knew she loved the Lord and held strong convictions, and I wanted to assure her that I wasn't some kind of playboy. But she'd also just graduated high school, and somehow, it came out sounding more like, "I may want to marry you at some point."

It struck Mary Beth as a little intense. She may well have gotten a mental image of being thrown over my shoulder and carried off to places unknown. Our dates stopped, but we remained friends.

A year went by. Mary Beth and I both dated other people and continued our ministries at the church. I sent her flowers and cards on special occasions. Occasionally, we wound up at the same social outings.

Then she called me out of the blue.

"What are you doing this evening?" Her voice revealed just a hint of something less than casual in it.

I was on pins and needles as we met for dinner. Always before, I initiated contact.

"I'd like for us to start seeing each other again," she said after we'd pushed our plates away.

I felt elated. I loved hanging out with her, and we had a lot in common.

We both grew up with strong, authoritative fathers and held conservative values. We both loved music and youth ministry and seriously wanted to serve God.

So I agreed, and our friendship quickly gave way to romantic momentum. After several months of dating, we discussed our feelings openly and knew we wanted to get married.

I intended to ask Mary Beth's father for permission to marry her. There was just one small problem: Right as we agreed to go forward with our plans, I ended up in the hospital with a kidney stone. Mary Beth's father worked as a corporate pilot and was about to fly out for a long trip. Meanwhile, I sat propped up in a hospital bed, recovering from surgery, rapidly tiring of eating Jello and clicking through the television channels.

"I don't want to wait," I told Mary Beth when she popped in for a mid-morning visit.

"We may have to. He's about to leave." Mary Beth sat next to my bed, squeezing my hand.

"When?"

"Tomorrow morning."

That was how I ended up asking my future father-in-law for Mary Beth's hand from a hospital bed.

"I'm in love with your daughter. I promise to take care of her always."

I meant it. But somehow, the checkered gown I wore took some of the punch out of my words. I recall the scene as clumsy and wildly humorous. I could imagine him saying, "I'm sorry, son, but I had someone more healthy in mind for my daughter." I also remember thinking that if he decided to beat me up, at least I would receive prompt medical care.

However, he consented, and we married six months later.

A few months after our wedding, our pastor asked Mary Beth and me to take over the youth ministry at the church. We were delighted.

Even as I pursued my career through college, the Pickens County Sheriff's Office and another local police department after that, I remained involved in ministry. Even if I'd tried, I could never forget what the traveling evangelist told me when I was a 12-year-old boy — about the ministry I would have writing and performing songs, of how I would reach many people with the Gospel. His words stayed with me all those years.

However, I wasn't ready to plunge into full-time ministry. I'd been raised in a hardworking, upper-middle-class family. I wanted my own American success story. As far as I knew, that meant earning six figures, having a healthy, happy family and a big house full of toys. The truth was that I desired material success more than I did serving God in ministry.

So, while I kept doing ministry on the side, I continued to pursue lucrative secular work. After several years as a police officer, I switched to construction work. I set out to learn everything about the industry and quickly advanced through the ranks by working ferociously. In the meantime, Mary Beth found employment at a bank, then later worked with deaf students at a local school.

Over those first 15 years of marriage, Mary Beth and I dug in and built our life together. We brought three healthy kids into the world — Coleman, Riley and Avery. Family life was sublime, and Mary Beth was a calm, steadying presence — a perfect counterbalance to my great bursts of energy and productivity. All the time, I continued to do youth and music ministry on the side.

In consideration of my father's suggestions, I started a home renovation business in 1999 and a new home construction company in 2003. Everything I put my hand to succeeded wildly. By this time, I'd learned a great deal about the building industry, and I poured every bit of my knowledge and energy into my businesses. The money flowed in unchecked, year after year, particularly through the housing boom that started in the early 2000s. We owned three homes, boats, cars, motorcycles, RVs — pretty much every material thing we could ever want.

I started to feel miserable. Between business, ministry and my family, I worked brutally long hours. All of it lost its luster. I found myself trapped in a meat grinder of my own making.

I got on my treadmill every night and prayed to God.

You have blessed me beyond my wildest dreams, Lord. I don't mean to sound ungrateful, but I'm unhappy. I've gotten everything I wanted, and I still feel like I completely missed the boat.

I prayed variations of that prayer hundreds of times over those years as I ran on the treadmill. My workouts functioned as several things at once: much-needed exercise (my work was mostly administrative by then), prayer sessions and, ironically, a graphic representation of my life — running like crazy and going nowhere. An outsider might regard that analysis as insane — I seemed to hold the world by the tail. But everything inside me screamed for something deeper.

I prayed and prayed but didn't recognize any response from God, other than an almost indiscernible whisper: *You know what you need to do.* I sensed God calling me to give up my extravagantly self-focused lifestyle. I knew we could make it on the spare wages ministers usually make. However, the idea of trimming down didn't appeal to me. I always pictured myself enjoying "the good life." It seemed like my birthright.

As all these thoughts tumbled about in my head day after day, I kept running and praying and hoping that somehow I could keep it all and get out from under the weight of my unhappiness.

Who wants to go back to the drawing board? Pushing

40, I did not desire to dismantle everything I'd worked so hard to achieve. Besides, I loved making six figures and having whatever I wanted. My wife and kids weren't complaining much, either. When offers came in to take over full-time ministry positions, I scarcely considered them. Most of the time, the positions offered almost no compensation.

It was a strange predicament to be in, because I *loved* doing ministry. Whenever I shook off the constant demands of work and went in to minister to the young people, or lead worship in our church, the inward screaming stopped, and I glowed with peace and joy. From time to time, complete strangers would tell me they sensed God had plans for me in the ministry. All of it echoed what the evangelist told me when I was 12. A quarter of a century later, those words still played in my head as though they had just been uttered.

The heartache went on for nearly a decade. Then, in 2009, everything changed when the housing market collapsed. Up to that time, my companies had survived the recession even as we watched work dry up for many of our colleagues. Now, however, the depth and intensity of the financial crisis couldn't be ignored.

My business partner was cautiously optimistic.

"Maybe this won't be so bad. The economy always bounces back. Let's not go crazy here."

"No, it's bad." I took a sip of coffee and scarcely tasted it. "We're looking at more than 10 percent unemployment. Banks are failing."

"We're still okay, though. We've got a year's work ahead. Surely things will look better in a year."

"Maybe. Projections say otherwise, though. At the very least, we have to think about downsizing."

The discussion went on. We prayed. We examined every angle. Nothing we proposed seemed satisfactory.

I felt more anxious than ever. As was my habit, I threw on a pair of sweats, climbed onto my treadmill and fired it up. An unfamiliar sensation came over me as I began to pray. Something inside me was breaking. For the first time in my life, I understood several things with complete clarity. First, I'd made money a priority over obedience to God. Second, I was essentially running my own life. And last, I was the cause of my own pain.

Pride has been called "the great sin." Anytime before that moment, I would have insisted I was living a godly life, but I couldn't claim that any longer. My own arrogance caught up to me.

Lord, this is it. I've been wrestling with you long enough. I know you've called me to ministry. I've felt the power of your presence as I've worked in ministry. I think I've been avoiding the obvious all these years. Now, I'm asking you to speak clearly. Whatever your answer is, no matter how difficult it may be to accept, I will be obedient. I'm trusting you with everything — my livelihood, my family, my time and everything I have. My life is in your hands.

The moment felt electric. It felt like a dormant part of my spirit came instantly back to life as I prayed. It was as if

TRUTH ON A TREADMILL

God said, *Okay. You know what you need to do. Now we can talk. This is the first time you've been willing to listen.*

I didn't need to have the rest spelled out for me. I knew in an instant that God was telling me to walk away. *Leave your kingdom, and begin working for mine.* It wasn't audible or explicit, but to me it was crystal clear.

Why did I wait so long to do this? I thought, as I kept putting my feet down on the treadmill — left, right, left, right. I leaned my head back and closed my eyes. I was overjoyed.

Suddenly, my foot hit the back wall. Without knowing it, I'd slowed my pace, and the track pulled me back toward the wall. In a second, I tumbled, trying to catch myself. But my hands only scrabbled at the air. The tether clipped to my waistband connected to a magnet on the machine. In the event of a fall, the machine should shut off when the magnet pulls away. But the tether separated from the magnet, and the treadmill continued spinning. My whole body flipped over and over, like being tumbled in a washing machine.

Finally, my ankle caught on the power plug and stopped the machine. I lay there sporting fresh bruises but completely at peace.

"I'm with you all the way on this." Mary Beth stood over me a little while later, inspecting my bruises and listening to my plan. "This is going to be great." She wore a huge grin.

That night, in place of our ordinary evening routine, we began an Internet search for full-time ministry positions in the area. We stayed up several hours, talking excitedly.

"What if God moves us somewhere else? We don't necessarily have to take a ministry here." Mary Beth tucked some hair behind her ear and worked the computer mouse.

"No, we don't. Just think — what if we end up in Florida or something?"

As we discussed the possibilities, we expanded our search.

Neither of us slept a wink that night.

ಿಲಿಲಿಲ

"Chris and Jeannie are moving to Alaska," I told my wife around a bite of scrambled egg.

"Why?"

"They've been hired by a church up there as associate pastors. They're doing the same thing we're trying to do."

We'd struck out on all our search efforts so far. It had been around a month since my revelation on the treadmill.

"Oh, I don't want them to go!"

"Me, either." Chris and his wife, Jeannie, were close friends.

"Why don't we fly up there with them and stay for a week?" Mary Beth suggested. "We can help them get settled in. We've never been there. I've heard it's stunning."

That's how we ended up in Alaska for an impromptu vacation, taking in soaring mountain ranges and vast stretches of pristine wilderness. We couldn't have imagined half the beauty that exists there.

A few days after our arrival, we were helping Chris and Jeannie move furniture into the parsonage when the pastor showed up. He'd come to speak with Chris but took time to speak with me as well. I ended up telling him my story, including my 10 years in the construction trade, my prayer on the treadmill and our current search for a full-time ministry position.

Two days later, the pastor of Chris' church asked me to go with him to visit another church in the area. Without much more explanation than that, I agreed, and off we went. Within a few minutes we arrived at the other church and ended up in a conversation with two of the associate pastors there.

"You know, we're looking for a full-time music pastor," Pastor Jeremy told me. "I think you would be a good fit. Why don't you stick around for another week, and see what may come of it?"

I liked Jeremy and his wife, Chareé, and humored them politely, but I initially thought there was *no way* we could possibly consider relocating our young family to Alaska. It was basically a different country. The church in question was in Fairbanks, which was geographically isolated and routinely experienced temperatures as low as -45 degrees during the long winters. Both Mary Beth and I were used to living in the hot South.

More polite conversations ensued with the other pastors there over the next few days.

Finally, I received a text from the lead pastor. "Why don't you just come out and lead worship for us next Sunday morning?"

I was sitting on my hotel bed the evening before we were to fly home.

"I appreciate the offer, but I'm getting on the plane in the morning."

"Well, why don't you stay an extra week?"

"I'd love to, but it would cost $400 to delay our flight."

"We'll cover it."

"I have a rental car and a hotel room to pay for. We weren't planning on any of this."

"We'll pay for all that."

"Well, there's still the matter of my business. There's payroll and logistics to be seen to. My partner is juggling everything back at home."

"Surely things will wait another week. Come on, you're running out of excuses here."

"Okay, but let's be clear about this. When we fly back to South Carolina, we're *never coming back.*"

"Okay. That's fine. If that ends up being your decision, go with our blessings."

So Mary Beth and I agreed and drove out to the church the following weekend. It was Easter Sunday. We prayed with the worship team before the service, then launched into the set of music.

After the worship finished and we took our seats in the

front pew, I sensed something significant happening. I felt joy so strong it was like my insides were burning. I knew we were supposed to move there.

I dreaded having to talk my wife into the move. I feared she would list a hundred legitimate objections.

"I felt the same exact thing," Mary Beth said, when I broached the subject.

"You what?" I was shocked.

"Yes. This is what God wants. I'm sure of it."

We spent the next several months shutting down the businesses and selling most of what we owned — all the business equipment, our RV, ATVs, cars, boat, motorcycle, televisions and electronics equipment. We found buyers for everything we attempted to sell. The only thing we kept was our cabin in the foothills outside of Travelers Rest, South Carolina.

We flew to Alaska with only a bit of baggage and some personal belongings. The church welcomed us warmly as I greeted them for the first time as the official worship pastor. It felt like coming home.

The next few years amazed and challenged us. Even though we embraced life in Alaska, it brought some hardship and adjustments. The five of us went from living in a 2,500-square-foot home with every convenience to living in a tiny one-bathroom parsonage above the sanctuary of a church. With so many changes, everything took on a surreal feel for a while. Everything our five senses took in was unfamiliar, except for the sound of each other's voices and the few belongings we had carried from home. We lived in a vast, snow-covered landscape with trees and bushes and wildlife we'd never seen before. We encountered more oddities than we could count — the feel of automobile tires sliding on the ice, people bobbing about swaddled in great thick coats, hats, boots and mittens, the exhaust coming out of our tailpipe in cloudy puffs because of the cold.

We loved it. The kids loved their schools, made good friends and enjoyed being in the thick of things by living right at church. For me, the experience of doing full-time ministry was better and more fulfilling than I could have imagined. The screaming heartache that had plagued me for 10 years was a memory. I sensed God telling me, *Aren't you glad you decided to trust me?*

As we learned to live frugally, we enjoyed every imaginable outdoor activity, including hunting and fishing, which supplemented meals on our tight budget.

Pastor McDonald encouraged me to return to school for a ministry degree. I applied at several schools and received an acceptance letter from the University of Chester at Mattersey Hall in England. I could take relatively short trips, attend a few weeks of seminar sessions and fly home to finish my course work and submit it by email.

So I flew across the Atlantic in the fall of 2011 to start my first round of intensive lectures. I'd never been overseas before. Going to England became the latest in a series of brand-new opportunities that arose with a seeming randomness. Although I believed God directed my path, it felt uncomfortable at times, to the point of pain. I often felt off-balance and occasionally longed for the familiarity of steering my own ship again.

But it wasn't to be. Events continued to unfold in ways that constantly challenged me. Two years after we arrived in Alaska, Pastor McDonald and the other pastors left the church, creating a leadership vacuum. I needed to take over all the pastoral responsibilities, including worship, preaching, counseling, baptisms, baby dedications, weddings and hospital visits — all while continuing my theological studies.

I cannot explain how I managed to do it all. Perhaps my body's requirement for sleep, rest and leisure were supernaturally diminished so I could meet each demand. The work brought my God-given gifts bubbling up out of me. I was in my element. I wasn't resentful or exhausted, though at the end of the long days, I often collapsed into sleep the moment my body lay down.

In 2012, Mary Beth and I began to sense a stirring to return to South Carolina and start a church in Travelers Rest. The message was strong, mutual and unusually specific. However, it seemed like a pipe dream. I hadn't yet finished my seminary degree. We had no means and could only imagine endless obstacles if we actually set out to obtain a property and seek volunteers to staff it. Besides, how would we draw in the people to form the congregation?

In spite of the obstacles, Mary Beth and I felt strong reassurances from God. As much as we enjoyed Alaska, we both longed to be back home. More than anything else, we dreamed about what God could do if we planted a church there.

We wanted this new church to be a place where people didn't feel the need to pretend, where the activities inside the building were as relaxed as everything we did outside of church.

As we planned, I often recalled a clever saying: "Religion is sitting in church thinking about going fishing; Christianity is going fishing and thinking about God." It was this kind of spirit that we wanted to prevail.

The transition was difficult, challenging and sometimes exasperating, but I was often reminded that we were helped by God, who had proved himself again and again over the prior three years as we ricocheted through various adventures. The calling we sensed to Travelers Rest became so clear that we turned down the opportunity to stay in Fairbanks as pastors at another church there.

We began the difficult process of searching for a church building in South Carolina. Everything we found was out of our price range. Then my father, who knew of our plans, called to tell me about an old church building that came up for sale. It needed some renovation, but the departing church planned to leave the PA system in place for the buyer.

"You can start having church right away," Dad told me over the phone.

It seemed impossible, but we sent the word out, and through a series of divine provisions, we secured a matching grant to purchase the property, which was right in Travelers Rest.

We were thrilled. This was really happening! However, some of our enthusiasm wilted after we made the two-week drive from Alaska back to South Carolina. We pulled into the parking lot and looked at our new church. It was a sagging, disheveled building on the inside with broken fixtures and stained, dingy carpet. Everything looked dull from lack of upkeep.

What have I done? I just turned down the opportunity to become the lead pastor of a thriving church and receive a regular paycheck. Now I had zero income, no people to preach to and a building that needed months of work.

I called a trusted friend who was in need of a church family.

"Do you want to start a church with us?" I asked bluntly after we sat down for coffee with Keith and his wife, Mae.

"Sure!" they said in unison, almost without pause.

We started working immediately. I drove out to the building every morning and began taking pews out and pulling up the carpet. Each evening, Keith drove out after work with take-out for dinner. We worked until we couldn't stand up anymore, then went home and returned to do it again the following day. Over the next five months, we refinished the original hardwood floors under the old carpet, painted the entire building, fixed sagging cabinet doors and anything that needed attention. Each Saturday evening, we dragged all the trash out from the week's work and carried a few pews back into the church so we could hold a small service the following morning.

At first, the services consisted of my family, plus Keith and Mae and a few other friends. Right away, however, we began to see other people trickling in as they got wind of us. To this day, I don't know how they learned about the church or why they wanted to come. I hadn't promoted the church in any way. We had no nursery, no coffee, no bulletins or any of the other standard accoutrements. We had only an idea that God had impressed upon us. But little by little, seven became 10, 15 and 20 by the end of the summer. The people weren't just coming for services. They were showing up to help with the work in the evenings as well.

We decided to call ourselves Upcountry Church, as Travelers Rest is in the northwest region of South Carolina known as the "Upcountry." We told people we knew that we were starting a church, since by this time we had finished the renovation, and on October 21, 2012, we had our first official service. Altogether, 126 people came, mostly friends and family members who traveled from out of town to support us. It was a festive affair, with balloons, banners and an after-service barbeque. The following Sunday, without the out-of-town visitors, 35 people turned out for the service.

This is what starting a church looks like, I mused. *Hasn't God been faithful so far?*

Mary Beth and I and the kids moved into the 850-square-foot unfinished cabin that sat empty since we left

Greenville for Alaska, and I finally finished my master's degree in theology. However, the financial demands of the church left us without a salary for the first year, during which we fed ourselves and paid our bills by cashing in our meager retirement accounts, selling what we could and accepting whatever gifts others gave us. I saw the hardship as a test. During the difficult times, I could almost hear God asking, *Did you really mean it when you said you would trust me?* I did, and we haven't missed a meal, though our standard of living is nowhere near what it used to be.

All this brought growing pains. My whole family felt the sacrifice, but the change has been overwhelmingly positive. Even though it meant uprooting the kids and asking them to start over in bigger schools and a much smaller house, they've taken the upheaval in stride. We love our lives together, investing in the church and serving others. God moved my affections completely from the material to the spiritual.

Over the years, it became clear that everything we went through prepared us for this. Out of the strangest of circumstances, and after building our entire lives on something else, God brought us to Travelers Rest and gave us a church family with whom we enjoy the most authentic Christian fellowship we've ever experienced.

After God gave us Upcountry Church, we resolved to make it a home for people who feel weary of the religious trappings found in many more formal churches. We have never felt compelled to water down the Gospel. To the contrary, what we have is a distillation of Biblical principles and our best church experiences.

Mary Beth and I gave up everything for this, literally. After we made that choice, we found our cups running over with far better blessings — things we never made room in our lives for before. This is the divine exchange — our self-centeredness and materialism replaced by God's peace and the joy of doing his work.

We watched people come to our church, give their lives to Jesus and grow before our very eyes. It is humbling and staggeringly beautiful at the same time. We have often heard people comment, "This is what we've been looking for!" We can't be the biggest or the coolest, but we can be absolutely real.

We never started a church before. Despite all our ministry experience, we often felt completely unqualified for this. However, from the start, we trusted in God's guidance, which taught us to focus on people instead of presentation and to make Jesus Christ the center and the ultimate focus of everything we do.

From humble beginnings, we continued to change and grow. Our philosophy, however, remained unchanged. The same message that moved me to choose full-time ministry became the subject of my first sermon in our new church building.

"There is nothing wrong with desiring a life of plenty. We serve a God of abundance. But it's a different matter to insist on it. All my life, in everything I did, I relied on my wits and my strength. It made no sense to give away 10 years of hard work. But God was persistent, and I was miserable living for my own idea of success.

"We shouldn't be afraid to trust God with everything. He has better plans for us than anything you or I could come up with. Let him in, and find out for yourself. Psalm 34:8 reads, 'O taste and see that the Lord is good. Blessed is the one who takes refuge in him.'

"Somehow, we don't really understand God's faithfulness until we have gambled everything on it. He wants us to see his provision up close and personal. I have seen it. My life is full and rich beyond my wildest dreams. I wouldn't go back for all the money in the world."

CONCLUSION

The stories you've just read may seem astounding to you. They certainly do to me, every time I read them. Something exceptional and uncommonly beautiful is uniquely woven through the fabric of each of their lives. What is it? God's love. The same astounding love God has for *you*.

Here's what else amazes me — realizing that every good thing each of us searches for can be found in him. Happiness, contentment, peace, true love — these gifts come from God alone. And the best part is, he wants us to have them all, in the deepest way possible.

We at Upcountry Church believe God has already written an exceptional story for *you*, too. A story where you live a completely fulfilled life. Honestly, isn't that what we're all searching for?

Of course reaching that destination and finding that true fulfillment does not mean that we are perfect. Far from it. At Upcountry, we know we're imperfect people. We're still on that journey. We've simply found our purpose in it, which is the difference between *wandering* and being full of *wonder*. We're all at different stages in our journey, yet none of us walks alone, because we have him, and we have each other. Indeed, one of our favorite parts of being on this path together is inviting others to join us.

FOUND

So please allow me the privilege of extending an invitation to you now. An invitation to meet the people in these stories and others like them, who would very much like to hear your story and to share a real friendship as we walk this path of life together.

Through the ups and downs, the good and the bad, and everything in between, we are stronger and better together than we are alone. That is what makes our Upcountry family so special. We are in it together, for the long haul.

You see, Upcountry Church is full of searching people just like you, who finally found what they were looking for. So please consider coming by. Stop in for a visit.

I also understand that perhaps your location or other circumstances might prevent you from coming to our church. The good news is you can still discover your purpose and find true fulfillment right where you are, because the answer to every human longing, the cry of every heart, is found in the person of Jesus Christ, and he is not limited by geography or circumstance. The only thing that can keep you from discovering new life in him is your own resistance. No other circumstance, no outside force, no other person can keep you from finding everything that you have been looking for in him.

The Apostle Paul said it plainly when he wrote, "Who shall separate us from the love of Christ? Shall tribulation, or distress, or persecution, or famine, or nakedness, or danger, or sword?" (Romans 8:35 ESV).

Paul asked this question because he knew the answer.

CONCLUSION

Paul had found what he was looking for, and he wanted everyone else to find it, too, so he offered this response to his own question: "… I am sure that neither death nor life, nor angels nor rulers, nor things present nor things to come, nor powers, nor height nor depth, nor anything else in all creation, will be able to separate us from the love of God in Christ Jesus our Lord" (Romans 8:38-39 ESV).

Paul knew the love of Christ, a love like no other, a love so strong that he (Jesus) allowed himself to die for each of us, so that we could break free from a life without purpose and live for something bigger than ourselves, something that transcends our daily routine and selfish ambitions. It is the life that we are all searching for, a life that can only be found in God the Father, through Jesus Christ, his son.

When asked by some of his friends how they could find their way to a truly fulfilled life, Jesus replied, "I am the way, and the truth, and the life. No one comes to the Father except through me" (John 14:6 ESV).

Becoming a follower of Jesus Christ is the path, the only path that will ever lead you to the life you have been searching for. And the first step in that journey can be praying a simple prayer of faith. A prayer that, when prayed with all honesty and sincerity, acknowledges our inability to create any lasting happiness or contentment for ourselves or anyone else. It is a prayer that admits our failures in trying to make it through life on our own, a prayer that recognizes Jesus Christ alone as Lord and Savior, the way, the truth and the life. It is a prayer that expresses our desire to be led by him, into the life that he created us to live, the life that we have been searching for.

When you pray that prayer, and open your heart and mind to him, you will be forever changed. For we believe it is in that moment that he places his own Spirit within you, to speak to you and guide you through this life. Never again will you have to be alone in your decisions, never again will you have to try and make it through another day solely on your own strength, because he will forever be with you.

So I've written a simple prayer for you here. Why not pray it to him now and finally find what you have been looking for?

Father, I can see now, after reading these stories and thinking about my own life, that what I've been searching for is you. I realize that all of my efforts to create a meaningful life on my own have fallen short. I know now that I need you to recreate me into the person you meant for me to be from the beginning. So I ask you to forgive me for everything that I've messed up in my life. Jesus, I believe that you died for me and that you are alive today and ready to change my heart forever. I know now that you are the way and the truth and the life, and so I'm asking you to be the Lord of my life. Come live in me, fill me with your Spirit and turn my wandering life into a wonderful testimony. I commit the rest of my life to you now, amen.

CONCLUSION

God hasn't given up on you. God never will. This can be the beginning of a new chapter in your story. So we hope to see you soon at Upcountry Church, to hear your story and together share what it means to finally be found.

Pastor Rob Rucci
Upcountry Church
Travelers Rest, South Carolina

We would love for you to join us at Upcountry Church!

Check out our Sunday morning service times at our
Web site: www.upcountrychurch.org.
Our address is
2 Church Street, Travelers Rest, SC 29690.

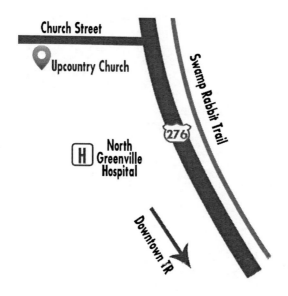

Please call us at 864.610.0699 for directions,
or email us at info@upcountrychurch.org.

For more information on reaching your city with
stories from your church, go to
www.testimonybooks.com.

GOOD CATCH
PUBLISHING